Stepping TwoGether: Building a Strong Stepfamily

Nancy Landrum, MA

With

Mary Ortwein, MSW

Dedication

To every couple who heads a stepfamily…
Who is longing for a way through the dark tunnel of endless issues,
Wondering if there is a map to guide you to peace and loving.
This is for you.

And to Jim…
You hung in there with me.
We made it through.
I'll am so thankful for my years with you!

I am grateful to…
Mary Ortwein, MSW, President of SkillsWork.com
You were the first invited me to create a curriculum to
teach step-couples these life-transforming strategies. You also contributed numerous
exercises and stories that enriched the program and this manuscript.

Multiple Researchers…
You refused the centuries-old assumptions of how it *should* be,
and instead looked for solutions that really work.
Bless you all!

Featured Step-Couples…
You have so generously shared your honest
experiences—the failures as well as the successes.
Thank you!

Thanks to Bradley Burck of Burck Communications for the lovely cover design.

PREVIEW

STEPPING TWOGETHER: Building a Strong Stepfamily

Most, if not all, marriages begin with blissful confidence surrounded by a soft cloud of romantic love and sexual energy. Ours was no different. We were euphoric. We didn't have a clue that a few short years later the paragraph below would describe our relationship.

> *Divorce! The word shattered the space and hung in the air between us like a red fog. Even after all the conflict we'd experienced, we were both stunned to silence by the introduction of that possibility. How could our relationship have come to this? Why wasn't it enough to love each other? We'd always heard that love and commitment were all it took to have a great marriage. We did love each other. We were very committed to each other and to our marriage. What was wrong? We'd both been through so much and were so happy to find each other. We were in our forties. Adults. Why couldn't we resolve the conflicts that were eating away at our love and commitment like a deadly cancer?*

The words above are the opening paragraph of **How to Stay Married & Love It! Solving the Puzzle of a SoulMate Marriage**, a book my late husband Jim and I wrote. (Available on Amazon.com)

OUR STEPFAMILY STORY

After only four-and-one-half years, my first marriage ended abruptly when I was twenty-three years old with the unexpected death of my husband. I had two boys, Steven who was two years old, and Peter who was eight months old.

Several years later, a mutual friend introduced me to Jim, a widower whose wife died after a protracted illness. He had three children: Teri who had married Greg a few months before I met Jim; Karen, a seventeen-year-old senior in high school; and Jimmy, his eight-year-old son. My sons were thirteen and fifteen years old.

We married in the Spring of 1981. We had each survived the loss of a spouse, were responsible, caring persons, and were sure that we were due for some better times. We had no doubt that we were meant to be together. After celebrating our wedding vows, we blissfully left for a two-week honeymoon.

The day we returned from our honeymoon, the conflict began. We had very different styles of parenting, and our ideas about what Jimmy, Jim's young son, needed were miles apart. Over the next few years, our hurtful communication methods exacerbated the conflict as we each grew more entrenched in our respective positions. The areas of safety between us began shrinking as the area of conflict expanded. We began to lose hope. Each of us secretly feared our marriage had been a terrible mistake.

In spite of our disenchantment, we didn't want to give up. Jim and I began an intense search for help. Eventually we found a great coach who taught us the basics of good, non-inflammatory speaking skills. We diligently began to use those. We began to take turns speaking and listening. (What a concept!) She also taught us respectful anger management skills.

We devoted ourselves to always treating each other with respect…and when we couldn't, we vented our anger safely away from each other. Each of these skills were *essential* to stop the fighting… halt the downward spiral…but they weren't enough to help us resolve the main conflict. We didn't know it at the time, but we desperately needed to understand the fundamental difference in dynamics between first families and stepfamilies in order to find a workable solution to our issue.

Our coach finally made a suggestion that was shocking to us, and painful to implement, but turned out to be a successful solution. You'll learn about this simple, research validated solution later in this book.

REAL SOLUTIONS WITH REAL STEPFAMILIES
In addition to illustrations from my own stepfamily, in this volume you will meet several step-couples, and a few of their children, hear their struggles, and learn from their successful solutions.

Comprehensive lists of **Building Blocks** and **Stumbling Blocks** to success will be shared following the introduction of each recommended strategy for success. These lists are gleaned directly from research that identified solutions to common stepfamily issues that work well for most stepfamilies and those solutions that were chosen by step-couples whose marriages eventually failed.

> **DEFINITION OF A SUCCESSFUL STEPFAMILY**
>
> A SUCCESSFUL STEPFAMILY is one in which the husband and wife are committed to learning and using respectful communication skills with each other, their children, and stepchildren.
>
> Their expectations are realistic.
>
> Solutions to issues accommodate the stepfamily dynamic.
>
> The marriage is strong and loving.
>
> Honor is given to the other living or deceased biological parents and extended family.
>
> The children feel safe, cared for, and respected by the adults in their lives and their stepsiblings.

You have no doubt noticed that I am using the old-fashioned term, stepfamily, vs the newer, more popular label of "blended family." I personally have a negative, visceral reaction to "blended family." We are not thrown into a blender and magically come out as a tasty, lovable treat. "Blending" does not usually happen in a stepfamily.

The term "stepfamily" was adopted in centuries past when marriages had an average length of seven years due to death from illness and accidents. When remarriage occurred, the new spouse "stepped into" the role left by the deceased spouse.

I accept that this is not an ideal term, but until there is one better, I remain committed to using "stepfamily" as the descriptive term of a marriage with children from a previous relationship.

NOTE: All stories from the couples and individuals cited have been reviewed and approved by them for inclusion in this book. When requested, fictional names have replaced real names.

BUILDING TASK

To the best of your ability, prepare yourself to have an open mind…what some call a "beginner's mind." Some of what you learn here will be new and perhaps, even threaten your current beliefs. Other things will make so much sense that you'll ask yourself, "Why didn't I see this sooner?" Everything shared in these pages has been validated by multiple research programs and then proven to work in the real families whose stories are so generously shared.

COMING UP…

You may be asking, "What's so different about stepfamilies?" In Chapter One you'll discover why the divorce rate for second or subsequent marriages is considerably higher than for first marriages…and what you can do to divorce-proof your marriage!

TABLE OF CONTENTS

DEDICATION
PREVIEW

Chapter 1: WHAT'S SO DIFFERENT ABOUT STEPFAMILIES?	Page 1
Chapter 2: MEET THE CAST	Page 6

NURTURE A STRONG AND LOVING MARRIAGE

Chapter 3: DO YOU HAVE THE MAP?	Page 15
Chapter 4: STEPFAMILY HOUSE-BUILDING TOOLS	Page 22
Chapter 5: NURTURE THE MARRIAGE	Page 33
Chapter 6: PARENTING TO SUPPORT THE MARRIAGE	Page 41
Chapter 7: MONEY MANAGEMENT TO SUPPORT THE MARRIAGE	Page 50
Chapter 8: THE EX…AND OTHERS	Page 54
Chapter 9: COLLIDING TRADITIONS	Page 61

NURTURE A SECURE CHILD

Chapter 10: MEETING THE NEEDS OF MY CHILD	Page 75
Chapter 11: THE HEALING POWER OF LISTENING	Page 85
Chapter 12: MAKING IT WORK FOR MY CHILD	Page 90
Chapter 13: THE "CRAZY" EX	Page 95
Chapter 14: PARENTING AN ADULT CHILD	Page 101

BUILDING A CARING STEP-RELATIONSHIP

Chapter 15: STEP-PARENTING	Page 107
Chapter 16: CREATING SAFE BOUNDARIES	Page 115

STEPPING TWOGETHER: BUILDING A STRONG STEPFAMILY

Chapter 17: MORE FROM THE CAST	Page 121
Chapter 18: STEPFAMILY KIDS SPEAK OUT	Page 127
Chapter 19: AN ONGOING PROJECT	Page 135

CHAPTER ONE: What's so Different About Stepfamilies?

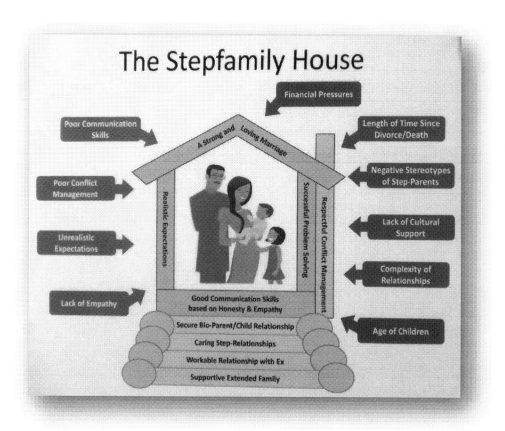

A STEPFAMILY HOUSE
The metaphor of a house embodies the image of a safe, stable, loving place in which to rear a family. Various components addressed in this chapter are compared to parts of a house that combine to provide shelter from the elements...a foundation, walls, a fireplace and chimney, a roof.

TEN STRESSORS
Researchers have identified ten primary stressors that hammer away at the structure of a stepfamily. Four of those stressors erode the stability of a stepfamily from within...like an active infestation of termites. A step-couple shares the corroding effect of these four stressors with first-family couples. These four stressors are (1) Poor Communication Skills, (2) Poor Conflict Management, (3) Unrealistic Expectations, (4) and Lack of Empathy (the ability to understand another person's point of view.)

The Foundation: (1) Good Communication Skills. Clear, respectful, non-attacking, speaking and empathic listening skills are the essential in any healthy, loving relationship. In many relationships, good communication disappears when presented with the stress of conflict. Stepfamilies are subjected to more sources of stress than first-families. The use of attacking language and poor listening exacerbates the conflicts in a stepfamily. Researchers identified (1) **Poor Communication Skills** as one of the primary stressors that lead to stepfamily (as well as first family) breakdowns.

A Functional Fireplace and Chimney: (2) Good Conflict Management Skills. All long term, close relationships have moments of heat...disagreements, hurt feelings, conflicts. Few of us are reared in families that model good conflict management. In childhood we learn to either hide from conflict, or win by intimidation. Because poor conflict tactics only get worse when under greater stress, and stepfamilies have more sources of stress than first-families, the need for practical conflict management strategies is even greater in stepfamilies. Research shows that **(2) Poor Conflict Management** skills are another primary cause of stepfamily breakdowns. Stepfamilies need a functional fireplace and chimney to safely handle the heat of inevitable conflicts.

A Structural Wall: (3) Realistic Expectations. There's no doubt that most of us marry the first time with unrealistic expectations hiding in the luggage we carry into our first apartment. Because stepfamilies have so many additional relationships and challenges inherent in their dynamic, the fall-out from unrealistic expectations is even more damaging. Our culture is remarkably lacking in knowledge or understanding about stepfamily issues. Most of us embark on stepfamily living with little to no solid information upon which to base our relationship behaviors. Choices are more often made from ego needs and/or an effort to look like a "real" family, (i.e., a first-family.) **(3) Unrealistic Expectations** was singled out as one of the primary stressors on stepfamilies. The balance of this book addresses unrealistic expectations that are unique to stepfamilies.

A Structural Support Wall: (4) The Need for Empathy. Some people are born with the gift of being able to see a situation from another's point of view...to feel the other's feelings. Some learn this skill from seeing it modeled in his or her childhood caretakers. You may have been instructed to "Imagine what she feels," or "He must really be hurting right now." The quality of every relationship is enhanced with Empathy. But for most of us *the quality of Empathy is in inverse proportion to how personally we feel threatened by a given situation*. More Threat=Less Empathy. Stepfamily situations frequently trigger us where we are most vulnerable... insecurities, fears, desires to be loved, wishing to be well-thought of, wanting to avoid failure. Stepfamilies often push us to the limit of our stores of empathy and require that we dig deeper. Research listed **(4) Lack of Empathy** as adding to the stress in stepfamilies. Empathy is a skill that can be learned or cultivated.

A Structural Wall: Effective Problem Solving. Although not singled out by research as a separate stressor, I'm including effective problem solving as one of the necessary skills that goes hand in hand with realistic expectations and good conflict management. The solutions to stepfamily issues are often counter-intuitive. Stepfamily solutions are usually found outside the box of our universal first-family model. In this volume you'll find examples of successful, effective problem solving. Note: *A successful solution is one in which both persons' core needs are met*. If only one person is pleased with the solution, it will eventually fail!

SIX ADDITIONAL STRESSORS FROM OUTSIDE THE STEPFAMILY WALLS:

Stressor #5: Lack of Cultural Support. The brains of everyone in the world seem to be stamped with the first-family model. In spite of each of us knowing many stepfamilies, our thinking and our culture tend to ignore stepfamilies' unique needs. One of the first places separated or divorced parents with young children notice lack of cultural support is in the school system. In spite of the fact that a large percentage of their students' parents live at separate addresses, school notices are sent home with the child. It's then up to the child or the custodial parent on that particular day to make sure the other parent is updated about events, grades, permission slips, etc. Some divorced parents are commendably communicative in regard to co-parenting their child. But many former couples, who lacked good communication when together, maintain their wars after separating, by refusing to share information about their child or, even worse, expecting the child to be their communication link.

Another place where lack of cultural support may show up is in the attitudes of extended family members. Grandparents, aunts or uncles may, rightfully, wish to maintain connection with their biological grandchild, niece or nephew with visits, special outings or gifts. The extended family members may not realize the hurtful impact on the step-sibling left at home. Or they may not realize the inequality of one family giving nice gifts while the step-sibling's family is totally uninvolved. Then there are those amazing families who seem to welcome all with open arms!

A third place you may notice lack of cultural support is when others—friends or acquaintances—either expect your family to look, act and feel like a first-family (and are shocked when you don't) or criticize you for solutions to issues that seem wrong to them because they don't fit the first-family model of a family. You may find the subtle, or not so subtle, pressure to conform to the first-family image coming from many surprising sources.

Stressor #6: Finances. Combining two families seems like it should reduce financial stress because usually it means also combining two incomes. But it rarely works out that way.

Most stepfamilies experience increased financial stress. Spousal support stops after the spouse remarries. Often child support *is* being paid. Sometimes child support is owed, but *isn't* being paid. Many step-couples enter marriage or cohabiting with debts from legal struggles hanging over their heads. Or new legal issues bring increased financial demands. Sometimes the new partner resents working to help pay for obligations belonging to the other partner's former relationship!

Stressor #7: Length of Time Since the Death or Divorce. For most, it takes between 4-7 years to fully regain one's balance after the trauma of the death of a spouse or a divorce. Yet most who remarry, do so within about two years. That short length of time before remarriage means that one or both partners are bringing unfinished grief from the loss and/or unresolved issues from the previous relationship with them into the new partnership. Launching a new relationship, and confronting stepfamily issues while still in a fragile state, means that there are fewer inner resources available with which to cope with unfamiliar and challenging issues.

Stressor #8: Age of the Children. Although not always true, as a general rule, the younger the child at the time the stepfamily is formed, the fewer the adjustment difficulties for that child, the parent and step-parent. A child entering puberty is already experiencing major adjustment issues. Adding a step-parent, step-siblings and, often a move to a new home and school to the mix, makes navigating puberty that much more difficult. A rule of thumb sometimes used is that it takes roughly twice the age of the child at the time of stepfamily formation, before that child is comfortable with the new family. For example, if your child was four years old when the stepfamily formed, that child may be fully integrated into the new family by around age eight. If the child is fifteen when the new family is formed, it may take until age thirty before that young man fully accepts his step-parent, if ever. And this assumes that the step-couple's marriage has survived and is strong and loving.

Stressor #9: Complexity of Relationships. Most of the step-couples interviewed for this book have relatively simple relationships. Each person has one Ex, deceased or alive, sharing custody or out of the picture. Among the family stories told in this book, Ted and Julie have the most complex family tree. In Chapter 2, they describe their histories. After Ted and Julie married, one of their children had to draw a family tree for a school project. He invented a fictional family tree, with their blessing, because trying to depict the reality of his complex history of relationships would be just too hard to draw, let alone explain. For those readers with similar histories, their story may be especially encouraging.

Many stepfamilies must cope with a complex web of extended family relationships similar to, or more difficult than Ted and Julie's. The complexity of relationships adds a significant amount of stress to an already taxed family dynamic.

Stressor #10: Negative Stereotypes of Step-Parents. Why do so many fairytales have a step-mother that's a wicked witch? Why are step-fathers universally assumed to be abusive? How often, in real life, do you hear of a step-parent being the hero in an adult's recounting of their childhood? Whether from real life examples or fictional characters, the negative stereotype of step-parents adds pressure to relationships that are already tentative.

There's no doubt that some step-parents exemplify the negative stereotypes. Otherwise the characterizations would eventually fade away. But many, many other step-parents, perhaps even most, do their very best to disprove the wicked image, and work hard to befriend and care for his or her step-child.

BUILD STRENGTH INTO THE STRUCTURE TO MANAGE THE STRESSORS:

It is totally within your control to mitigate the negative effect from all ten stressors. You do that by learning better skills for communicating, managing the strong emotions triggered by stepfamily issues, adopting realistic expectations by reading about the experiences of other step-couples, practicing great problem-solving skills based on stepfamily research, and developing a deeper empathy for the experience and feelings of your partner and the children in the family.

SUMMARY
Whew! With all of these stressors it's no wonder that some step-couples fail to make it through the first few challenging years. Even with reasonably good communication and conflict management skills, somewhat realistic expectations and a decent degree of empathy, it takes from four to seven years for a stepfamily to stabilize. Many step-couples crack from the strain, giving up when, with the addition of some core skills and realistic expectations they could make it through to, not the perfect family they imagined, but to a functional, loving family.

The successful step-couples whose stories are told in this book worked hard to learn and strengthen skills that reduced the impact of the ten stressors identified by research. By using good communication methods, practicing respectful management of conflict, adapting expectations to fit stepfamily dynamics, adopting solutions that work for most stepfamilies, and stretching your abilities to be empathic, you, too, can build a safe, stable structure that provides shelter from the stressors that attack your stepfamily.

Today there are more supportive resources for couples attempting this heroic feat than there were when Jim and I began our journey together. Several are listed in the back of this book in the section titled **Resources.**

BUILDING TASK: Identify Stressors

Look back through the list of Ten Stressors that defeat so many stepfamilies. Label each with a number 1-5. The number one is assigned to stressors that are having little negative impact on your stepfamily. The greater the impact, the higher the number assigned with five representing a severe and desperate impact on your partnership or on your child. How does it feel to know you are not alone? That the agonizing struggle you may be experiencing is somewhat normal for stepfamilies? That there really are solutions that will help you as a step-couple and your children break through to a happier place?

COMING UP…

In the next chapter, meet the couples who share their very real stories throughout this book.

CHAPTER TWO: Meet the Cast

The concepts that help stepfamilies succeed come from research that identified practices common to many stepfamilies who thrive. But concepts can be confusing or dull. It's sometimes hard to know how to apply concepts to *your* situation. So, woven throughout the presentation of concepts will be the true stories of several step-couples and their children. Their words and experiences will make the facts live and breathe. Their experiences will help you see how to apply the concepts to your own cast of characters, because as you read the following pages, you will see yourself, your partner, your child, your stepchild, your parents, your extended families, and your Ex.

In this chapter you'll hear a little of the history of these step-couples and children. As you hear their stories in the following chapters, you'll be able to track their struggles, and their progress. The book ends with updates about them, the quality of their relationships now, and their advice to you.

IT'S PERSONAL WITH ME: Jim and Nancy Landrum
You read a brief history of my late husband Jim and I in the *Preview* to this book. Everything I write about is personal, borne out of my own journey of heartbreak, learning and triumph, but it's especially true of our stepfamily journey.

Because of the loss of my first husband at such a young age, my goal was to enjoy a 50th anniversary with Jim. Knowing that, on our 7th anniversary, Jim took me out for a wonderful dinner and gave me a beautiful, romantic card. He signed it, "Here's to forty-three more years!" I smiled and thanked him, but inside I was saying to myself, "Forty-three more years! I don't think I can last that long!"

Shortly after that, the help we'd been seeking began to appear. First, we learned some better communication methods...speaking more respectfully and actually listening to each other. We also learned some critical anger management tools. The combination of those skills stopped the fighting. Six months later we resolved the parenting issue that had brought us to the brink of divorce. We also learned to keep our agreements with each other—an absolutely essential component to rebuilding our trust in each other. With the rebuilding of trust, and the giving of respect, our feelings of love returned, multiplied times ten!

Jim and I accomplished what I still consider one of the most difficult and rewarding feats of our lives, the resurrection of our failing marriage and the bonding of our stepfamily. We came so close to giving up. We nearly let the ghouls and goblins of fear and immaturity, ignorance and ego, defeat us. But we didn't. After nearly eight years of painful conflict, we treasured the following seventeen years of peace and joyful love. Relationships with our children and step-children became more loving, respectful and loyal.

Our success led us to teach other couples the skills that enabled us to save our marriage. The classes we taught led to my return to school for a Masters Degree in Psychology. Shortly thereafter we published **How to Stay Married & Love It! Solving the Puzzle of a SoulMate Marriage** and began speaking at national conferences and a local stepfamily support group.

When Jim was diagnosed with terminal cancer, and subsequently died in 2005, I thought my days of speaking, teaching and writing about relationships were over. But after the fog of grief began to clear, I discovered that there was nothing else I wanted to do. The lessons we'd learned were so compelling, and the need of many couples for reliable help was so great, that my journey as a teacher, author, and coach has continued.

In one major respect, Jim and I were fortunate. We did not bring into our marriage the wounds of a previous, failed relationship. We did not have to cope with hostile former spouses, demanding former in-laws, or an impersonal legal system dictating custody arrangements or visiting agreements. I can only try to fathom the additional stresses that those factors place on the already fragile structure of a stepfamily. Thus, I am especially appreciative of the step-couples who share their stories here.

The couples whose stories follow, I met as participants in the classes I taught 2007-2013. I am so very proud of each of them and grateful that they've consented to have their stories illustrate **Stepping TwoGether: Building a Strong Step-Family.** Their words are taken from interviews conducted by me.

TED and JULIE (They requested fictitious names)

> Ted and Julie first met in the 5th grade in 1980 and quickly became best friends. Even when they went to different high schools, they made time to hang out together on weekends. When they graduated from a *Mastering the Mysteries of Stepfamilies* class in March 2010, they had been married for four years. They each had two children from previous marriages. This interview was conducted about six months following the beginning of their implementation of stepfamily guidelines in their family. I share their relationship history here because their backgrounds and circumstances are more traumatic and complex than the other interviewees and may be an encouragement to some readers.
>
> **Julie:** Ted (with his then girlfriend who became his first wife) came to my first wedding when I was 23 years old. Although several family members and friends expressed their concerns about my choice, I went through with my marriage to Tom. Abusive behaviors began only two weeks after the wedding. It began with name calling and throwing things, graduated to breaking things, then to hitting me, pulling the telephone cord out so I couldn't call police. It continued with financial tyranny and infidelity with my best friend. He made sure we only owned one car and prevented me from attending school. He wanted total control. Our son, David, was born in '93 and Susie in '95. They were three and five years old when I left with a police escort after he'd chased me around with a buck knife.

I met Cole on line, a firefighter from Mississippi. He seemed very kind. He came to Mississippi to visit me and the kids. We soon married. My Ex surrendered his parental rights to avoid child support payments. My dad convinced Cole to adopt David and Susie because the court wouldn't allow me (the mother!) to have sole custody.

My marriage to Cole was never very intimate. He liked that I was raising his kids for him, even home schooling them. He brought a check home and spent every night he was home drinking in the garage. He eventually reunited with a high school girlfriend and said he didn't want to be married to me anymore. He just moved out. Neither of us was sorry. He gave me 6 ½ years of safety. It helped me regain my balance after being afraid for my life with Tom.

Ted: I met Carol at college and married her in spite of her noticeable problem with drinking. During our first few years she attempted suicide several times. We split before our son Thomas was a year old. One night I was sitting in my apartment when I got an urgent, sick feeling in stomach. I drove straight to where Carol was living. I could hear the car running in the garage. When I opened the door, she was unconscious. I turned the engine off, called 911 and found Thomas in his crib with a suicide note. I took custody of Thomas at that time. I was making great money in my business, and was caring for Thomas, but was a dad on the fly.

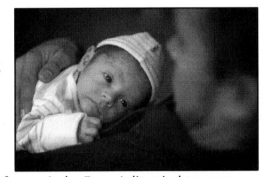

I met Kim at an escrow company. My family told me I was out of my mind. Even Julie tried to warn me. Kim quickly became verbally and emotionally abusive to two-year-old Thomas. One time he dropped a piece of rice on the table and she freaked out. She'd throw his toys in the trash. She repeatedly said, "He's not part of *our* family."

Meanwhile Thomas's mom had gone through counseling and re-hab. She wanted to spend time with Thomas—reconnect. I wanted Thomas to know his mom, so I shared time with her even though I had custody.

Kim and I had a baby girl. The birth was difficult, so I was very active in taking care of Annie. I felt very bonded with her.

After Annie's birth, Kim became even more abusive to Thomas saying, "Now we have *our* family." Kim was so rejecting and abusive with Thomas that when he was with me, I'd take him to my dad's or a hotel. She wouldn't allow any photos of Thomas in the house. The court would not allow her to be present during any time I spent with Thomas. In spite of that, one time I allowed her to drive with me to pick up Thomas from his mother's. On our way home she began to be angry. She wanted a reaction from me and I wouldn't engage. She turned on Thomas and began screaming at him. "I wish you were dead! You're the reason we're in so much trouble!" When we got home, I packed a few things and left. I was so tired. I began praying, "God, please help me!"

Annie was only 3-4 months old when I left with Thomas. I was so bonded with her, but because of her age, the judge only allowed me two hours per week. I left the courtroom sick to my stomach. I knew that as she got older, I'd get more time. I was a single dad uninterested in another relationship. I was just doing my job, spending some weekends without kids and some with kids. About three years went by. I was resigned to being a single dad. There was not one person I could imagine wanting to see until Julie emailed me out of the blue.

Julie: A friend saw Ted being interviewed on television for his business. I looked up his company's website. I had no idea whether he was still married, so I just sent a general, "How are you?" email, not even sure if he would answer.

Ted: I was sitting at my desk at work. It was a shock to open Julie's email. I replied, "I'd like to come see you and see how you're doing."

Julie: We hugged and cried and had a great visit. He came out again….and again. I knew he was serious because he's afraid of flying and I was still in Mississippi.

Nancy: Why did either of you think you could have a sane marriage after these horrendous relationships?

Julie: The only thing that sounded familiar and comforting was our friendship. Ted was the only person in the whole world I knew for sure loved me and I loved him. We both thought we were finally going to do it right!

Nancy: How long did it take to realize it wasn't going to be easy?

Ted: When we returned from our wedding trip, I was facing two court battles, one each for Thomas and Annie. Thomas's mom was drinking again in his presence. He'd come home and tell me what was going on. She was neglecting him. Once he called me crying. She ripped the phone from him. I was trying to get him protected. Kim took us to court for *everything* about Susie. One thing would get resolved then the next week I'd get court papers regarding something else.

Julie: Add conflict between Ted and me to the mix. We were fighting over the parenting of our children. Ted is very structured in the way he parents. I am far more relaxed. Ted's family told him to leave me. When he refused, they broke off all contact with us. We were spiraling downward. Very little could be discussed. We had fights in front of the kids, about the kids. We had no dates, no time for us. Everything had become a competition. My kids had had no contact with their adoptive or biological father since 2005.

Ted: In 2007 after my last court appearance with Thomas's mom she won back the right to share custody. Two weeks later she was diagnosed with brain cancer. A court mediator was appointed to watch over him. Soon I was given full custody of Thomas because his mother's health was deteriorating. We assume she died, although her parents, Thomas's grandparents, have resisted all efforts to stay in touch.

Thousands and thousands of dollars had gone into court battles—paying attorneys right and left. Meanwhile the economy tanked and I lost my business, other investments and a million-dollar home. My car was repossessed. We couldn't afford to put gas in our family car. We moved twice.

Julie: We knew we still loved each other underneath all the chaos, but we'd lost trust in each other. Both of us had been in insane relationships for so long. Yet, we both believed that God was with us individually and still had a plan for our lives. We also had our memories of our very solid friendship as children. Even though we'd lost each other for a while, Ted was a safest place I'd ever known.

Ted: In January the church where we attended had a preview of all the marriage classes offered for Spring.

Julie: At the preview, we heard a woman talking about her experience in a stepfamily. She (Nancy Landrum) was promoting *Mastering the Mysteries of Stepfamilies* class. We related to everything she said. The minute the meeting was over we went to her and poured out how desperate we were for help.

Ted: Although the class didn't start for four more weeks, Nancy had experienced the desperation of hanging on by her fingernails, hoping for help. She agreed to see us a few days later. After listening to each of us describe what was happening from our respective points of view, she asked if we were ready to take steps for immediate relief. We would have done anything at that point! We loved each other and were heart-broken that we couldn't seem to make our marriage work. Without doing something differently, we were teetering on the brink of another separation.

Nancy: *More of Ted and Julie's story will be shared in future chapters as you hear the skills and concepts they employed to bring their marriage back from the brink.*

KIP and WENDY

Kip and Wendy had each been divorced once when they met and fell in love. At the time of this interview, Kip and Wendy had been married for four years. Their original wedding date was postponed by a year while they prepared themselves for the challenges of stepfamily living. Kip has four boys. Wendy has two girls and a boy. They are active leaders in their church's Remarriage Program.

Nancy: Why did you postpone your wedding?

Wendy: We were supposed to be married in October, 2004. Somewhere around May or June we realized there were some areas of conflict we needed to resolve. We postponed indefinitely. By the following April or May we were ready to set a firm date.

Kip: It was a hard year...one of the hardest we've had. We both thought, "Are we actually going to get married?" Some issues had come up that hadn't been apparent the first year we were dating. But that year was also one of the best years! During that year we were really pushing to work through the issues that had been exposed by the classes we took and the counseling sessions we had. The communication course we took was so helpful.

Wendy: We knew we had a lot of differences but we weren't able to identify the differences out in the open and didn't know how to work on (resolving) them. We (worked with a therapist and) took personality assessments, etc. We learned about temperament and male/female differences. In the process we understood why certain things we did with each other triggered old junk. Once I was able to understand, I didn't get upset quite so easily. It's a combination of learning to communicate better and understanding our differences through the assessments we took. We were in pre-marital counseling for the 2004 wedding and stayed with it through the next year that we were struggling to move forward. We really learned a lot about ourselves and each other through that process.

Nancy: *You'll hear about how Kip and Wendy resolved their parenting and financial differences in future chapters.*

CHARLES and CAROLE (They asked that their names be changed.)

Charles was widowed with three children when he met Carole, divorced with two boys. Charles was career military. Carole worked as a government analyst. They dated for a year, and at the time of this interview had been married for nine years. At the time of their marriage, Charles's two daughters were seventeen and fifteen years old, his son was eleven. Carole's two boys were five and ten. For one period of time there were four teens in the family.

<u>**Nancy: How was it to have four teens in a new stepfamily?**</u>

Charles: Not easy. It wasn't quite like commanding a battalion in combat, but close. When we got married we knew that we would have to do some work. We'd thought about *some* things, but I'd say that it's impossible to anticipate how much work it's going to be. It takes a tremendous amount of effort! Having some knowledge ahead of time would help, but we did "discovery learning"—meaning that we discovered what we needed to learn as we went along.

Nancy: *How Charles and Carole managed financial differences, a difficult Ex, and unaccepting grandparents are shared in future chapters.*

JANELLE and ARMANDO

Janelle and Armando had lived together for seven years but were reluctant to commit to marriage because of their frequent arguing. The constant conflict was even creating health problems. They wanted to stay together, but knew they needed to do something different in order to achieve the quality of relationship they desired.

Nancy: *In CHAPTER FOUR you'll see what happened when they learned skills that enabled them to stop fighting and commit to marriage.*

KEN and IRMA

Ken and Irma had each left a previous marriage. They both had children from those unions. Most of their children were grown and gone except for Ken's twenty-something son. They vowed they would never divorce again.

Yet, they fought so ferociously that they eventually divided their home down the middle with black electrician's tape, even going so far as to divide the refrigerator space! They laugh about that now, but it really wasn't funny at the time!

Eventually they attended a class where they learned better ways of communicating and resolving their issues. They were so excited about what they learned, and the great results they got, that they have been teaching others those skills in multiple classes ever since.

I met and worked with them when we were both working for a non-profit organization that taught relationship skills to lower income couples all over California. When I developed **Mastering the Mysteries of Stepfamilies** curriculum, they co-taught classes with me.

You'll hear more about how these step-couples overcame the unique challenges of step-family building in future chapters.

THE EXPERIENCE OF TWO STEP-KIDS

NATHAN

Sometime after his parents divorced, his mother lived with, and eventually married Ken. He spent the balance of his childhood in this stepfamily along with a step-brother. He attended **Mastering the Mysteries of Stepfamilies** in order to better understand the (sometimes) crazy stuff that went on in his home.

SUSIE

Recalls the traumas of multiple changes in her family and shares her determination to avoid a stepfamily experience of her own!

SUMMARY

Statistically in America there are more stepfamilies now than first-families. Yet so little is commonly known about the unique challenges of stepfamily dynamics. The divorce rate for second (or subsequent) marriages is higher than for first families. These couples could have been included in those dismal statistics, but, instead, they recognized the need to learn new skills and choose creative strategies in order for their marriage to remain strong and loving...and their stepfamily to thrive. They give you practical, real solutions that enabled them to resist the ten common stressors that too often crush the hopes of step-couples.

BUILDING TASKS: Be Teachable

We are trained from birth to achieve independence. Most two-year-olds include "Do it myself!" in their first attempts at speaking in sentences. Stepfamily stressors wreak havoc with your ego. It seems like it should be simple...obvious...how to make this new love stay alive and this new family work for all. But the simple and obvious often turn into devastating and ongoing conflict. Be willing to learn from the concepts shared and the examples given by these courageous couples.

Coming Up...

Examine **Unrealistic Expectations** more thoroughly in the next chapter.

STEPPING TWOGETHER: BUILDING A STRONG AND LOVING MARRIAGE

The strength of the marriage is what ultimately defines the success of the stepfamily. The greatest portion of this book, therefore, is dedicated to the practices that enrich and nurture a strong, loving and lasting marriage.

CHAPTER THREE: Do You Have the Map?

Let's pretend. You, Tony, have applied for and been accepted as a contestant in one of those crazy reality show contests…something like *The Great Race*.

You and your daughter are still recovering from being in a train wreck. You're a little disoriented. But the prize if you win this race is safety, security, love and happiness for you and your precious daughter.

At the staging area for the beginning of the race you meet Trish. She is recovering from a similar trauma—the infidelity of her husband. She has a son. Trish, also desperately wants to win this race for the prize—safety, security, love and happiness. The two of you decide to partner-up, believing you have a better chance at winning together.

You've packed for the journey. Your children are coming with you, so you describe to them what an adventure this will be. You introduce yourselves to each other's child. Both children seem a bit subdued, a little shy, but as you each hold your child's hand, you take a deep breath and prepare to embark.

The host of the show hands out the instructions in unmarked envelopes. Together, you open the envelope, take out the instruction sheet, and read, "Go to Successful Stepfamily Township. There you will find safety, security, love and happiness. Good luck!"

That's it. Nothing else. No map. No directions. The only vehicle you have has "First-Family Bus" written in cold letters on the sides.

You look at each other in bewilderment. Where is Stepfamily Township? How do you get there? Where do you start? *When* you start, how will you know you're going in the right direction? Tony's little girl is hungry and begins to fuss. Trish's son senses the confusion and acts out his insecurity by running around, yelling annoyingly. You both stand there, looking at each other, thinking that the other contestants must have gotten clearer instructions.

Nevertheless, they gather their things and get on the only bus they see, the one labeled "First-Family Bus."

Shortly Tony says, "In a normal family, the mom and dad share the responsibility for the children. Your child is out of control. I think he needs more discipline."

Trish responds defensively, "It's true I haven't quite known how to channel his energy, but he's a good kid. Don't be too hard on him. And, by the way, your daughter has you wrapped around her little pinky. All she has to do is cry and you give her whatever she wants!"

After a short distance, Tony discovers, "Your finances are a mess! I had no idea you had so much debt. Shouldn't some of this be paid by your Ex?"

Trish replies, "I couldn't afford a very good divorce attorney. Now I'm stuck with the credit card debt from my previous marriage. And while we're talking about money, why do you pay so much child support to your Ex when your daughter is with us more than half of the time?"

They each begin to wonder, "If I'd chosen a different partner, would he/she have known how to reach Successful Stepfamily Township?"

And so, the stepfamily journey begins...

UNREALISTIC EXPECTATIONS: A Supportive Wall

Most marriages start out with some unconscious unrealistic expectations. The common ones are expecting your partner to know what you need without telling him/her. Another one is expecting that you'll be in peaceful agreement about everything. Or, believing that you're so much in love that there will be no rough patches...or at least that you'll work them out with ease. If you were reared in a stable family where Mom and Dad worked things out, you have a much better chance at mimicking their success. Or, you are smart enough to find a class that teaches you the skills for respectful communication and effective problem solving.

In the case of step-couples, you want the same destination that first-married couples want. In fact, because of the trauma in your past, you probably desperately want a happy marriage and stable family for yourself and your children...but don't know how to get there. You have a map that you think will help you arrive at safety, security, love and happiness. You are unaware that the map was intended to help first families achieve that goal. When this map is used for a stepfamily journey, it will only lead to another train wreck and multiple disappointments.

Most step-couples begin their journey being unconsciously set up for problems because of the first-family map ingrained in our culture. A few months after launching a new stepfamily, or a year or two down the road, many step-couples find themselves feeling trapped, lost in a bewildering desert where cactus and rattlesnakes threaten every relationship, every encounter. You desperately want this marriage to work. You are doing the best you know how to do for your children, and stepchildren, but the family is unraveling at the seams. Some kids are acting out. You are fighting over a variety of issues...or maybe just one main issue. Other kids are hiding out in their rooms. You began the journey believing that you could create a happy, healthy, loving family. Now that dream seems a cruel joke. A trick. How did you get *here* when you started out so full of love and hope?

Most often the reason is because you only had a map for a first-family destination. First-family map coordinates cannot deliver you to Successful Stepfamily Township.

WHAT IS THE FIRST-FAMILY MAP?

The family structure with which the world is most familiar is created when a couple dates, falls in love, chooses to cohabitate or marry and eventually gives birth to, or adopts a child, or children. This family structure is known as the "first-family" or "nuclear-family" model. The first-family model is deeply engrained in our collective unconscious as the way...*the right way*...to create a family.

First-couples usually get a honeymoon. First-couples get to engage in passionate sex within the walls of their first home. First-couples get to "play house" for a while before the realities of sharing a life creeps in. Yes, there are adjustments. A messy person marries a slob. Someone who loves order and predictability marries someone who thrives on spontaneity. The youngest child in the family of origin, accustomed to being pampered, marries a partner who's been independent and self-sufficient since the age of eighteen.

Most first-couples work their way through these adjustments with compromises, or fights, but find some level of satisfactory resolution. The first-couple map may often include a counselor, clergy member or wise confidante who reinforces the couple's commitment to each other and the relationship. Some first-couples are aided by map coordinates such as learning better communication skills, conflict strategies, adjusting their expectations and having some level of empathy for each other.

Most first-couples expect their finances to be joined, to work together toward shared goals, to plan vacations together, to invite extended family members to birthday parties, etc.

Couples forming a first-family have weeks, months or years to cultivate their love before adding the joys and responsibilities of parenting a child. And, usually, only one child at a time is added to a first-family. First-couples are emotionally connected to their children. They naturally expect to co-parent. Even though one person may assume major responsibilities for baby care, rides to pre-school, sports practices and supervising homework, both parents care deeply about the welfare of their child.

First-couples also have an image of what a successful first-family looks like. Their image may be romanticized and somewhat unrealistic, but nevertheless, it's a valuable image to aim for...a goal that's been reinforced by centuries of committed first-families. That first-family image is supported by love stories, both real and fictional (think of best sellers by Nicholas Sparks and Nora Roberts,) by grandparents married for sixty-five years, by parents who stuck it out through tough years and still love each other, by paintings like Norman Rockwell's famous family scenes.

IN CONTRAST...

Couples forming a stepfamily have some predictable things in common. We are exhilarated by another chance to have a "real" family. We long to find happiness for ourselves and our child/ren. Our expectations are high. We're tired of hurting. We're scared, but buoyed up by new love and soaring hopes. We dream of a loving, romantic relationship. We imagine our kids loving our choice of a new mate. She may believe that this man will help her parent a difficult child, or provide a healthy, male role model. He may believe, with all of his heart, that this woman has enough love to heal his, and his child's wounds. Even the children may be caught up in the excitement generated by new love, hoping that, at last, the dream of a happy, loving, stable family will be realized.

Many step-couples find their dreams are soon challenged, however, when their high hopes collide with the complex realities of stepfamily dynamics. In contract to the first-family who eases into the long-term commitments of family life, forming a stepfamily is a little like jumping off a high-dive into the deep end of a frigid pool of water.

At least one child, and often more, are already with you. (Rather than waiting to be born when you're ready for them.) From the beginning of the journey their needs, their difficulties in adjusting, concerns about those children must be considered. Usually there is an Ex, or two, that has to be consulted before any plans are made. Each partner comes with either assets or debts that impact the quality of life experienced. Each partner already has formed a parenting style, or has strong opinions about how parenting *should* be done.

Often one partner (and his or her child) move in with the other partner, creating resentment about "moving over to make room," or a sense of not feeling welcome or at home.

Nancy: We took the equity from the sale of Jim's house and doubled the square footage of my house—a mistake. The home was functional and beautiful, but my children never surrendered emotional ownership of the house, and Jim and his children never really felt like it was theirs. Sometime later, we learned that it works better to move into a new residence that is neutral territory for everyone.

Step-couples come together following the death of a previous partner or after experiencing the break-up of a previous relationship or marriage. Often, at some level, one or both partners are grieving the previous loss. Frequently there is leftover baggage from a painful breakup. In a stepfamily, one or both partners have a child from a previous relationship. Most of the time there are Exes, custody, visitation rights and extended family members whose rights and/or demands must be taken into account.

UNREALISTIC PARENTING EXPECTATIONS

Nancy: You may remember from the PREVIEW that my late husband Jim and I experienced our first fight over a parenting disagreement the day we returned from our honeymoon. True, it was only a little spat, but it soon morphed into frequent, real fighting. Our parenting styles were so different…and of course, we were each convinced of the rightness of our respective styles.

Julie: When I told Nancy that I just wanted a man who would love my children, she replied, "It's too late to have a nuclear family. That time is gone. You're in a stepfamily now and most stepfamilies only succeed by functioning with different (parenting solutions) than first families." It hit me hard. I grieved the loss of my first-family dream. I grieved the loss of a loving father for my children. I cried off and on for two weeks. (In a later chapter you'll learn more about how the love developed in this family.)

STEP-DOGS? REALLY?

Susan: When we first got married, both sets of kids were very territorial about their respective family dog. They were incensed that I expected the two dogs to share a water bowl! Even now when Charles's son and my son come home from college, Daniel takes *his* family dog out for a walk and Tim takes *our* family dog. It doesn't seem to occur to either one to take out both dogs!

Julie: My kids and I had two dogs, Rover and Sheba. They were a part of our family.

Fast forward six plus years. I found myself moving back to Southern California to marry the love of my life. The most difficult part was uprooting my children and all they had known. I love my dogs and I love my kids and my kids love the dogs and I just didn't see leaving them behind. I compromised quite a bit by making my daughter re-home her rabbits and one of her guinea pigs.

Ted wasn't an animal person. He wanted the dogs to stay outside. I agreed because the weather was milder in Southern California than it was in Alabama. But the dogs were very unhappy with their new outdoor paradise. They whined and scratched the door wanting inside. Within a month or so they were inside for just some of the daytime…which turned into night time…which turned into sleeping on our bedroom floor.

Ted reluctantly gave in quite a bit considering that, even to this day, he's not a dog lover. We laugh about it now, but there were times when there wasn't a lot of laughing going on. I never thought of a dog coming into the house as being such a big issue...but I also had never really been around anyone who wasn't a dog lover. It was new territory for both of us.

Nancy: Lady, our exuberant boxer, had been a full member of our family for about eight years before the Landrum bunch joined us. Lady loved the extra attention, but my boys resented Jimmy calling her *his* dog. I was hurt by Jim's irritation with her shedding and fleas. I accepted the extra vacuuming and flea treatments as part of the price I willingly paid for her valued membership in the family.

The first Christmas we were all together, Teri, Jim's oldest daughter, had married the year before. In a grand effort to give her support to the new family's first Christmas, she made each family member a red Christmas stocking. They were filled with fruits, nuts, little gifts and each was topped with a small package of gourmet Famous Amos Chocolate Chip cookies. The stockings were stored in a large brown grocery sack in our bedroom, waiting to be hung over the fireplace.

Jim and I returned home late one evening to find a trail of empty stockings, oranges, and nuts from our bedroom to the doggy door at the other end of the house. Jim was furious! He found Lady shirking in the shadows of the patio, fully aware that she was in big trouble. Torn Famous Amos wrappers testified to the fact that she'd eaten every cookie from every stocking. As he marched around the yard picking up bits of evidence, he was yelling in a heavy stage whisper to avoid rousing sleeping children or neighbors, "BAD DOG! VERY BAD DOG!" I knew he wanted to swat her but didn't dare. I was in the house, chuckling. He spent the next several days tracking down identical packages of cookies so he could reconstruct the stockings. They were outrageously expensive, but he didn't want Teri to think we were uncaring or unappreciative of her efforts toward family solidarity. It was many years before he would tell Teri the story and laugh.

Lady lived with our family for five more years. After her death everyone missed here, but no one grieved her loss more than Steven, Peter, and me. We had bonded with her as a puppy, and had eight more years of history with her than the Landrum half of the family.

OTHER SURPISES

Nancy: I remember the shock of going from cooking for three to cooking for six. After the first few weeks I thought it would help if I got organized. So, I made six weeks of menus with corresponding grocery lists. I planned to make large portions so that two nights a week we could have left-overs. It didn't occur to me that a man, three teens and an active boy would consume so much food that there was never anything left-over to give the cook a night off!

I expected my life to get easier now that I had a SoulMate, lover, and best friend with whom to share responsibilities. I thought my days of repairing sprinklers, installing curtain rods, or disciplining strong willed boys by myself were over. I thought my boys would be happy for me, not sullen and resentful. Jim believed his girls would be my friends and Jimmy would welcome me as "mom."

As these things didn't magically happen, another deeply hidden unrealistic expectation began to surface. I believed that my first attempts at "family" were flawed. I thought I'd lost my chance to be a truly great wife and mother because my first husband died, taking my dream with him. I had done the best I knew how to do as a single mom, certainly giving it all I had to give, but now I had a second chance! I want to *make this family perfect!* Because I didn't have healthy communication skills or an understanding of what makes a stepfamily work, I did what I knew how to do: I planned elaborate birthday celebrations; I cooked grand meals; I shopped for great gifts. I expended a huge amount of energy on how the family looked from the outside. I guess I believed that if we looked good, the inner bonding and love would follow. Instead, the wounds, resentments, and unmet expectations corroded our chances from the inside.

For me, as well as Julie, a large part of the healing was grieving the loss of the family I *thought* we would be. We would never be a "normal" family. I again, had blown the chance to be a perfect wife and mother of a perfect family. It's taken time and distance for me to see that there are *no perfect families*. Maybe there are no *normal families* either. There are just families…biological, step-, happy, sad, dysfunctional and healing. Grieving the loss of the *fantasy* made room for the wonderful *reality of the family that we became*.

SUMMARY

The brain-map of a family that most of us have in our heads is meant for a first-family. The destination that many step-couples try to achieve—to look, act and function as though they are a first-family—is usually impossible. Trying to reach that unrealistic goal is what causes too many step-couples and their children untold added stress, and sometimes delivers another relationship failure. One of the crucial components to a successful stepfamily is to identify and release your expectations that are based on a first family model. And Then learn about, and base decisions on realistic stepfamily goals.

This chapter looked at only a few of the unrealistic expectations that cause conflict in many stepfamilies. Future chapters will address other issues and suggest workable solutions.

BUILDING TASK: Identify and Release Unrealistic Expectations

This is not a one-time event. As you move through your step-family journey new unrealistic expectations will probably emerge that need to be exchanged for more functional beliefs.

For instance, when Jim died, the dynamics again shifted in the family. Whenever I see or speak to my step-children, the love and respect we worked so hard to make characteristic of our relationships are still there in spades! But we don't see each other as often as we did when Jim was alive. He seems to have been the hub around which our family revolved. My son and his step-siblings still love each other, and often make great efforts to be present for big events like the weddings of each other's children. But we no longer vacation together…or regularly have family gatherings.

As you read this chapter, what concepts challenged your beliefs regarding your stepfamily? Are you currently experiencing a conflict that could be the result of an unrealistic expectation? What personal comments did you relate to? What are you feeling now? Relief that you're not alone? That your experiences are not the result of your failures? Grief that your first-family dream may not be realized? Hope that as you continue reading you may find some solutions that work for you?

COMING UP…

In the next chapter get acquainted with the tools needed to build a strong stepfamily house.

CHAPTER FOUR: Stepfamily House-Building Tools

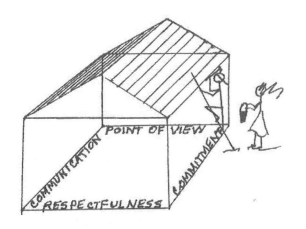

THE PROTECTIVE ROOF OF A STRONG AND LOVING MARRIAGE

The ultimate stability and function of the stepfamily depends on the quality of the marriage relationship. If the marriage is full of conflict and unhappiness and ultimately fails or just struggles along, it affects everyone else in the family. There is no question that building a strong and loving marriage is much more difficult with the added stresses and complex relationships in a stepfamily. But it is NOT impossible!

It just takes more of the same skills it takes for a first marriage to thrive. *That's why most of this book provides support for the marriage.* When the marriage is solid, the issues regarding the child and the step-child are much easier to manage.

This does not mean that the marriage is a higher priority than the safety and wellbeing of your child. You brought this child into the world and into this family structure. The real needs (not every demand) of this child to feel safe, important, and valued by you must be met.

One couple had spent time and effort learning good communication and conflict management skills. Those skills were helping them manage their own relationship with more respect. The woman had a 13-year-old son. Her husband, this boy's stepfather, thought that she wasn't disciplining him firmly enough. He wanted her to turn this child over to him so he could "make a man out of him." He was verbally abusive, demeaning and disrespectful to the boy. Wisely, she refused. The young man was depressed and expressing suicidal thoughts. She packed up herself and her son and got the boy to the counseling help he needed. The marriage did not survive.

One of the most difficult things about being an adult couple with children and step-children is juggling the needs of each of these relationships. It requires great "housebuilding tools" as well as patience and often selflessness. Your partner is not all yours. He/she also "belongs" to his or her child/ren.

More will be said about meeting the needs of your child in the section about parenting your child.

THE FOUNDATION: GOOD COMMUNICATION SKILLS

"We need to communicate better" is the self-diagnosis that most of my couple-clients say when they first come to see me for coaching. Just last night in a first appointment with a couple, they described a couple of major issues that, if resolved, would make their marriage happier for both. But they volunteered that if they could just communicate better, they'd be able to resolve those issues in a way that works for both of them.

If you and your partner learn, grow, and ultimately thrive through the challenges of a stepfamily, you gain the prize of a relationship you can count on and your child/ren will benefit from the model of a loving, respectful marriage.

Although every relationship can benefit from good communication and conflict management skills, step-couples and their children are particularly at risk without them. The best communication and conflict management skills I know are taught in **How to Stay Married & Love It!** The skills related in that book are the foundational ones that Jim and I learned and then scrupulously practiced that stopped the downward spiral of fighting that nearly took us out. Another option is the online self-paced program entitled **Millionaire Marriage Club.** (Found at www.nancylandrum.com)

As stated before, I'm not going to re-teach those skills here, but rather give a brief summary of them.

Speak to be Heard: After food, water and air, I believe that our deepest human need is to be deeply seen, heard and understood. Nothing is more emotionally satisfying than for someone important to you to really get who you are, understand how you feel...not necessarily agree with you, but understand. Words, gestures, tones of voice and facial expressions are incredibly powerful. Without meaning to, you may be using communication methods that practically guarantee that your message won't be received very well, and may be completely rejected. Learning how to deliver the message in a way that increases the chances of being heard and understood is one important goal of good communication skills. You and your partner may want to take The *Communication Tools Quiz* at the end of this chapter to evaluate the current communication methods you are using.

A SUPPORTING WALL: EMPATHY

Listen to Understand: Too often, when a partner or child is speaking, we are formulating a rebuttal, or selectively hearing one piece but ignoring the rest. Some, who've been conditioned to fear conflict, are looking for the nearest exit, or creating their own exit by emotionally withdrawing. Learning to focus on the task of really listening to the other person, for the purpose of thoroughly understanding what he is thinking, feeling, desiring, is a powerful skill that can transform most interactions.

With the skill of Listening to Understand, the listener repeats back what was heard in his or her own words to make sure the listener is understanding the speaker accurately. The speaker then verifies that the message was heard correctly, or restates it more clearly. Listening with the goal of understanding does not require that you agree with what is being said.

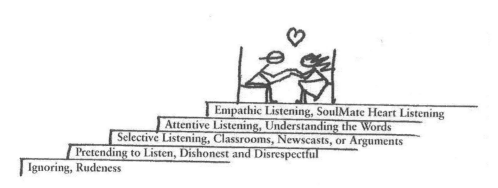

Listening to Understand works best when the listener is willing to temporarily *become* the other person, understand her thoughts and feel her feelings. This is the experience of *empathy*, one of the primary qualities identified by researchers as lacking in stepfamilies that fail. Empathy is a skill that can be learned, and one of the ways to learn is to practice Listening to Understand.

THE MAGIC COMBINATION: A Skilled Discussion

Discussion is defined as "an exchange of ideas or opinions on a particular issue with a view to reaching an amicable agreement or settlement."

A **Skilled Discussion** is dramatically different than an unskilled discussion! Unskilled uses manipulation, interruption, blame, silence or volume which often turns the "talk" into an escalating argument, hurt feelings and emotional distance without a satisfactory resolution ever being reached.

In order to safely and effectively talk about a touchy issue all major communications experts agree that *structured method of conversing has the highest rate of success*. A **Skilled Discussion** is when the speaker and listener patiently and respectfully take turns, alternating the roles. The "rules," or structure of a **Skilled Discussion** function like a seat belt and shoulder harness while driving—they keep both parties safe.

Combining respectful speaking and empathic listening in a **Skilled Discussion** has transformed many of my clients' heated conflicts into a softening attitude and greater willingness to work on mutually agreeable solutions. A successful **Skilled Discussion** naturally takes the communication from more surface levels (where fights take place) to the deeper levels of meaning and understanding that bring about greater intimacy and facilitate solutions that satisfy both persons.

In a **Skilled Discussion**, the speaker holds something that helps both parties keep track of who is the **Speaker** and who is the **Listener.** The concept is similar to the American Indian's practice of a Talking Stick. Although the **Listener** also speaks, he or she only speaks to repeat back the message sent by the **Speaker**. This practice insures that there is only one speaker at a time (taking turns being the Speaker) rather than having two speakers and no listeners. Discussion that have two speakers and no listeners often escalate into hurtful arguments!

Another essential rule is that *only one issue is addressed* in each **Skilled Discussion**. This prevents the downward spiral of one issue leading to another…to another…until nothing is resolved.

Learning how to have a **Skilled Discussion** and then practicing that skill is essential for managing the unique challenges of every step-couple. The guidelines of a **Skilled Discussion** are included at the end of this chapter.

Ted and Julie About Learning Skills:

> **Ted:** A few weeks after meeting Nancy we took her class. The first full Saturday of class went by so quickly! We were learning how to hear from each other's point of view. We heard each other with deep empathy, **Listening to Understand** (repeat back to the speaker what was heard.) It was transformational!

> **Julie:** I learned why my communication methods were creating and escalating conflict. I learned how to say, "I feel hurt when you…." rather than "You are so thoughtless!" That day and in the evenings to follow we grabbed and used every skill and concept that was presented in class. We were so determined to have peace and save our marriage and family that we practiced constantly. We put into practice the **Problem-Solving Skill** with issues that had been hot topics for four years, such as how much money we spent on our respective children.

Ted: We'd have to call time outs sometimes, (when emotions were too hot to stay in the format) but we were successfully talking about things that we'd tip-toed around in our efforts to avoid more fights. Decisions were being made that satisfied both of us. We've been successful in following through with our plans. Every successful **Skilled Discussion** was a miracle that we celebrated!

Julie: The love we knew was buried under everything has returned in force. We've gone on romantic dates! We have rediscovered why we've been friends through all of these years. The kids have calmed down. The whole family had been divided in half, but now relationships between the kids are healing. There is laughter in our house again!

Kip and Wendy's Process:

Kip: Initially we learned (better communication skills) from the *Couple Communication* curriculum. (www.couplecommunication.com developed by Sherod and Phyllis Miller.) It has some similarities (to the skills taught in *Mastering the Mysteries of Stepfamilies*) in that you repeat back what the speaker has said and share thoughts, feelings, etc. It was a real breakthrough for us. *It gave us the tools we didn't have to work through issues.* One of us would say, "Let's schedule a time to use the (Discussion outline) to talk about this issue." We also had the format on little cards so we would sit in a restaurant and take turns moving through our thoughts, feelings, concerns and desires while the other repeated back what had been said. In the beginning we used it a lot, but after a while it became more ordinary to speak and listen like that. When we recently took *Mastering the Mysteries of Stepfamilies*, **Listening to Understand** helped us go even deeper by putting ourselves in the other's shoes—imagining what it is like to *be* the other.

The biggest benefit to me (for doing all this work) is that now I know without a shadow of a doubt that whatever comes up we can work it through. Before, because of my personality, I was fearful of bringing up issues. Wendy is not afraid to voice her opinions or concerns. Since learning these skills, I don't feel like I have to hide in the corner anymore! Now, I just say, "Let's set aside a time and work this out." I know that we are both committed to working anything out *and* we have the tools to do so. We both wish we had these skills before our (first) marriages failed... but we have them now.

Wendy: The next level of communication with *Mastering the Mysteries of Stepfamilies*—the process of going deeper and putting ourselves in the other's shoes—refined the tools we had.

Janelle and Armando:

Janelle: The classes were very difficult at first, but we were committed to completing it. There were times when Mando did not want to attend the class but he wanted to see what the outcome might be. The outcome laid a foundation for our marriage!

Mando: (The skills we learned) gave us a platform to be able to discuss differences of opinions, conflicts and everything we desired without the fear of being judged or rejected. We learned that he who holds the (talking) stick has the right to speak and the other has the assignment to listen.

Janelle: We also learned to speak with love and respect even in times of distress. We learned to listen with the goal to understand. It's not a one-time fix but it's a continuous readjustment (using) the right tools.

Mando: We are able to talk about any issues. We are better listeners to Janelle's teenage daughter Janine. As a result, we have made a better home environment.

A year later, Armando and Janelle were wed, and soon after, welcomed baby Jasmine to their family. My latest update from them includes a family portrait that includes three daughters now!

Carole adds:

Carole: I think we could have done a much better job. I love Diane Sollee's comment: "We take classes for everything except our marriages." We could have benefitted from a marriage class that taught better communication and problem-solving skills. Usually couples in love think they don't need communication classes! (Diane Sollee's website is rich with relationship information and resources. www.SmartMarriages.com)

Jim and Nancy:

Nancy: We originally learned a very basic version of the skills these couples describe. But even so, for the first time we were able to talk about our very hot issue without the "conversation" escalating into a fight. After about 45 minutes of laboring our way through what we later called a **Skilled Discussion**, correcting ourselves when I was sarcastic, or he used the finger-pointing "you" message, we were exhausted. It was very hard…like it must be to speak in a new foreign language…but the results were the first hope we'd felt in months! We agreed to pick up the conversation again the next day.

As we stood, Jim held his arms open to me and said, "That felt so respectful. Let's do our best to always treat each other with respect." I agreed. We also agreed to ask the other for a redo if either of us slipped into our old bad habits.

A few weeks later, we looked back on that day as the day our marriage began to heal. *We never had another fight,* although it took a few more months of using these skills before we agreed on a solution to our main issue. That experience of success gave birth to our "Respect 24/7" policy that I've been teaching to clients ever since.

THE FIREPLACE: Conflict Management

There is a line that goes down the middle of every relationship. On one side are respectful words, tones of voice, facial expressions and gestures. On the other side are disrespectful words, tones of voice, facial expressions and gestures. It is a very definitive line. The more time spent on the respectful side, the more loving, trusting and nurturing the

> WHATEVER YOU CAN'T COMMUNICATE ABOUT CONTROLS THE RELATIONSHIP.

relationship will be. The more time spent on the disrespectful side, the less chance there is that this relationship will meet the deepest needs of either person.

It is realistic to expect that, in every close relationship, there will be circumstances that trigger strong emotions in one or both persons. Conflict management skills help you manage those strong emotions in ways that help you heal personally, and that keep you on the respectful side of the line in relationship with the other person. One basic skill is to call a "time out" on yourself when you know you are in danger of becoming disrespectful. Time outs have guidelines that prevent them from being manipulative or punishing to the other person. Time outs are relationship savers!

Healthy conflict management skills are one of the major requirements in order to build and sustain a healthy marriage and stepfamily!

Because there are so many potential issues that trigger conflict in stepfamilies, it's tempting to blame the issues—or the people who represent the issues (children, Exes, etc)—for the fights. The truth, however, is that the conflicts over issues only expose the weaknesses in a couple's communication and conflict management skills. One of my favorite relationship authors, Gary Smalley, says, "There are no problems that cannot be resolved. There are only people who will not resolve them." And I add, "Or don't know *how* to resolve them!"

Another favorite relationship teacher confidently states that "Conflict is growth trying to happen." (*Getting the Love You Want* by Harville Hendrix)

I particularly love this concept: "Conflict is the doorway to greater intimacy!" Conflict alone won't do that, but having the skills to successfully resolve conflict definitely increases intimacy, bonding us closer together.

Jim and Nancy:

> **Nancy:** Anger management was one of the most important skills for Jim and I to learn. We were accustomed to just blurting out whatever came to our minds, using many of the poor skills we later listed on the Communication Skills Quiz. (At the end of this chapter.) The predictable results were hurt feelings, escalating arguments, and increasing hopelessness about our relationship.
>
> Our coach introduced us to the concept of venting…letting off toxic steam harmlessly. She told us that healthy venting is done away from the object of the anger, and without hurting anyone else or anything of value. (Several examples are listed at the end of this chapter.)
>
> I like to write, so when I was too angry to speak respectfully to Jim, I would grab my journal and write everything I wanted to say to him, using any language I wanted. Eventually I'd calm down and be able to return to a Skilled Discussion with speaking and listening that was respectful.
>
> *Because we taught these skills together for eleven years, I can confidently repeat what Jim told our classes…*
>
> **Jim:** I don't like to write. So, I bought a mini-cassette recorder. When I was too mad to be respectful to Nancy I'd drive to a nearby park, sit in my car, turn on the recorder and tell Nancy off! I'd rewind,

listen to what I'd just told her, and say, "Furthermore…" and vent some more until all the poisonous anger was drained away. Then I could go back to Nancy and speak respectfully about our issue.

Sometimes I'd go to a golf course and hit a bucket of balls pretending Nancy's face was on every ball!

Nancy: We agreed that Jim would never read my journals and I would never listen to his recordings!

Anger is literally like poison in our bodies. It must be discharged. But there's no excuse for spewing angry, hurtful words and actions toward your loved one, or any other being, human or animal…or valuable property.

An acquaintance used "dish therapy." She'd buy cheap dishes at a thrift store, and when her anger with her husband was about to explode, she'd go into their back yard and throw the dishes against the concrete block wall yelling any epithets she wanted to while watching the dishes shatter.

Anger is normal. Venting anger out of the body with actions that are harmless to yourself and others is an essential skill. Adopting a healthy venting method is even more critical in stepfamilies where the added stresses often trigger anger.

I doubt that most of us have witnessed healthy methods of venting so it seems contrived and foreign to us. It's far more "normal" to just tell our loved one off, or withdraw in cold silence, behaviors that further damage the relationship. Healthy venting protects the relationship while releasing the toxic energy of anger from the body. The added benefit is the healthy model of emotional management you demonstrate for your children.

SUMMARY

I love this oft-used quote by Albert Einstein, "The problems we face cannot be resolved at the same level of thinking we were at when we created them." A common paraphrase of that quote is "Insanity is doing the same thing over and over again but expecting a different result."

Jim Landrum said it best, "Learning to communicate well requires practice, persistence, and patience, but the pay-off of a great marriage is worth the effort."

BUILDING TASK: Evaluating Skills

You may find it helpful to make two copies of **The Communication Tools Quiz** at the end of this chapter. Both you and your partner fill it out separately. If you then review each other's scores, don't get hooked into arguing about how you evaluated each other. Just see it as a neutral picture of where your communication methods are now and what those methods may be doing to prevent the relationship you want. Many of us aren't aware of the words and behaviors we demonstrate in a relationship that contribute to the negative results we experience. When you fill out this inventory, what surprised you? Were you shocked at your score? Did you find it easier to add up your partner's score rather than be truthful about your own?

You can learn these transformational skills by enrolling in the online course, **Millionaire Marriage Club**. Learn about the Club and enroll at www.NancyLandrum.com Learning the skills online has the advantage of needing no baby-sitter, moving forward at your own pace, and having the lessons available for repetition as needed.

Included are all the chapters of **How to Stay Married & Love It!** given as assignments in various modules, an audio recording of each lesson, and a Game that you and your partner can play that will reward you for practicing the new skills.

COMING UP...

There are simple practices that nurture a strong and loving marriage and are equally effective for children and step-children.

Communication Tools Quiz

Taken from the book, "How to Stay Married & Love It!" by Nancy Landrum
0=Never   1=Rarely   2=Sometimes   3=Frequently

Assign the most accurate number for your exchanges in the past 14 days.
Add up your score, your spouse's score and then a total combined score.

I do:	Partner does:		I do:	Partner does:	
___	___	Use "always" and "never"	___	___	Use accusatory "you"
___	___	Give unwanted advice	___	___	The silent treatment
___	___	Withdraw with hurt feelings	___	___	Use sarcasm
___	___	Blame	___	___	Make excuses
___	___	Heap on shame/guilt	___	___	Talk hopeless talk
___	___	Condemn in vague generalizations	___	___	Act like "poor me"
___	___	Slam doors/break valuable things	___	___	Run from conflict
___	___	Sidestep issue (i.e., change subject)	___	___	Be subservient/ passive
___	___	Insist on being in control	___	___	Call derogatory names
___	___	Refuse to assume responsibility	___	___	Bring up old business
___	___	Emotionally disconnect	___	___	Defensiveness
___	___	Compare spouse to another	___	___	Use hurtful humor
___	___	Jump from issue to issue	___	___	Embarrass in public
___	___	Use disrespectful tone of voice	___	___	Yell, scream, rage
___	___	Use threats in an attempt control	___	___	Lie
___	___	Punish by withholding affection	___	___	Intimidation/Violence
___	___	Use disparaging physical gestures	___	___	Hurtful targeted insults
___	___	Act condescending/ self-righteous	___	___	Get others to take sides
___	___	Threaten or flirt with infidelity	___	___	Force sex
___	___	Be unfaithful	___	___	Practice an addiction
___	___	= Totals	___	___	=Totals

Total of my two columns_____ + Total for partner's columns_____ = _____Grand Total
(Possible total of 240. Higher the total=higher the conflict, lower the satisfaction.)

In day-to-day life, we make constant course-corrections based on feedback—one key doesn't work so it must be the other one—but we seldom look at the feedback from (the results produced by) our communication methods. *Every* communication is an attempt to convey thoughts, feelings or needs and can be evaluated by this standard: Does it result in more or less loving, a better or worse relationship?

Insanity is doing the same thing over and over again but expecting a different result!

"Learning to communicate well requires practice, persistence, and patience,
but the pay-off of a great marriage is worth the effort."
Jim Landrum, How to Stay Married & Love It! Solving the Puzzle of a SoulMate Marriage.

Copyright 2002, Jim and Nancy Landrum. Copy for Personal Use Only.

Respectful, Effective Communication Guidelines

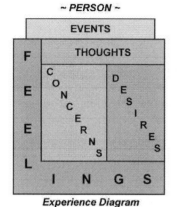

Experience Diagram

Speak to be Heard:
Set a date for any Skilled Discussion. It can be "now" or "at 7 p.m. this evening." But a time set apart and agreed to is one of the requirements for a successful Skilled Discussion.

Speaker: Hold a "talking stick" to signify that you are in the speaking role. Start with something good about your partner...an appreciation, for instance.

Listener: Repeat back the positive words spoken about you by your partner.

Speaker: Speak from your own point of view
 "I think (believe)... I feel...I'm concerned about...I want..."
 Remember the three word rule... I feel _____

Avoid use of absolutes like "always" and "never"
Avoid trigger words...words you know will incite hurt or defensiveness...or derogatory tones of voice.

Listener: Listen to Understand:
- Set aside your own thoughts, feelings, concerns and desires for the moment.
- Become your partner, seeing the world/issue through his or her point of view.
- Listen, not just to the words, but to the information given through facial expression and body language.
- Repeat back what you understand has been said using your own words.
- Try reading "between the lines," repeating back what may not have been said, but which may be true for the Speaker.
- Accept his/her correction gracefully.
- Use the thumb and index finger signal if you need information in smaller bites.
- Place your hand over your heart as the signal that you wish to speak.

Skilled Discussion:
- Trade places periodically. When the **Listener** becomes the **Speaker**, he/she takes the talking stick. On your first turn as **Speaker**, start with something good.

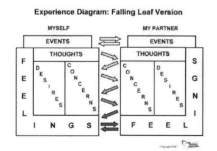

Watch for the Falling Leaf Effect.
- As each person is heard with empathy, the sharing tends to go to deeper levels of communication. The deeper the sharing, the easier it will be to decide on a solution to an issue that meets both person's core concerns.

- **Always end the Discussion with words of appreciation to each other.**

_{Diagrams are used with permission from Orange County Healthy Marriages Coalition and are not to be reproduced except for your own use.}

SUMMARY
1. Decide on only *one* topic to be discussed in this Skilled Discussion.
2. Make a date: specific time to have this Skilled Discussion
3. The person most eager begins as the Speaker.
4. The Speaker holds a Talking Stick (any object).
5. The Speaker begins by sharing something good about the Listener.
6. The Listener repeats back the thoughts, feelings, concerns and desires with the intention to fully understand the perspective of the Speaker.
7. Speaker and Listener take turns, developing a rhythm or pace that works for them.
8. Notice the *Falling Leaf Effect*. (Communication becomes more vulnerable with safety.)
9. Discussion is complete when both parties have shared from all sections of the *Experience Diagram and* both feel heard and understood.
10. Use the Problem-Solving Worksheet to work out the details and provide accountability for following through. (Request from Nancy)

This process is used with permission from IDEALS of Kentucky.

IDEAS FOR VENTING STRONG EMOTIONS:

- Write out your anger in a nasty letter. Then burn it.
- Speak your anger into a recording device. Then erase it.
- Do a heavy cleaning job with the intention of working off your anger. The kitchen? The garage?
- Use "dish therapy." Buy cheap dishes at a thrift store. Yell and break them until the anger is discharged.
- Scream into a pillow. Use any nasty language you want to.
- Beat the mattress or a sofa with a plastic baseball bat or swimming noodle. (I needed this one once!)
- Go for a long walk or run.
- Play a physically strenuous game like basketball.
- Pull weeds (one of my favorites.)

Note: Do not do any of the physically or verbally violent things in front of anyone, especially children. The angry energy being expelled may frighten them. Venting is a *solo* exercise to unleash the toxic energy of anger from your own body and emotions so that you can, then, go back to the relationship to *respectfully* work out the issue. This process may be used for angry feelings toward anyone, including your children and stepchildren, not only your partner, or for any other strong, toxic emotion like fear.

CHAPTER FIVE: Nurturing Your Marriage

Although the skills outlined in CHAPTER FOUR are the strongest foundation for any successful stepfamily, there are some other essential components, as well. Like the foundation of good skills, these components add richness, depth and intimacy to any relationship. In the (sometimes) chaotic events in a stepfamily, it is especially easy to become lax about these behaviors. Things like expressing appreciation, acts of kindness, dating, etc., help us keep our *main* focus on the good in each other, rather than zeroing in on the areas of struggle.

APPRECIATION

Have any of us ever gotten too much appreciation? My take on appreciation is that there is a world-wide famine—most of us are starving for recognition of our achievements or even just our attempts to do the right thing, validation that we're important, or acknowledgment of kindnesses given. It costs us nothing to give a word of encouragement or appreciation, yet some lives have literally been transformed by kind words spoken at a pivotal time. Because creating a healthy stepfamily requires so much energy and effort, being generous with appreciation to our spouse, our child and step-child may go a long way toward developing cohesive relationships.

Carole: I appreciate Charles's commitment and willingness to grow and adapt and be loyal...it all fits together. I appreciate what a great role model he is for my children. I have big worries about how they view marriage and women because of what they see from their dad, so I *really* appreciate the example Charles sets. He is very hard working. His willingness to learn and develop has facilitated our working through our issues. He follows through on commitments...does whatever it takes. It's not easy. I know how hard it is to change behaviors!

Charles: I could say about Carole all those things she said about me! Carole is persistent and won't give up on something she's committed to. It took a while and it's a continuous process, but I appreciate her acceptance of me with all my baggage—some of which she didn't see before we got married! Along with that, what I love the most is not only *her* ability to grow, but her ability to help *me* grow. She motivates me to change behaviors that have been habitual for 20-30 years by realizing that I don't have to stay the same. When it works to our advantage, I can change. For instance, I went to military schools...was in the military. We tend to be Type As with big egos. Carole's helped me see the positive side of being very forceful and confident, but also helped me recognize that a big ego can be very destructive to a relationship if not managed.

Nancy: We made the 300-mile trip to see my son Pete's graduation from the California Highway Patrol Academy. When Jim said to Peter, "Your father would be so proud of your today," it brought tears to Peter's eyes...and mine.

Growing up, I was rarely complimented. So, when Jim would give me a compliment or appreciation, it would kind of slide by me, off into the ether. I was a little uncomfortable receiving it. He finally took my face in his hands, looked into my eyes, and made me repeat the appreciation back to him. That repeating-back step (like in a Skilled Discussion) helped me internalize the gift he was giving me.

APPRECIATION EXERCISE

Every day for the next week, look for something your partner, child or step-child (or all three) has done well, tried to do well, a kindness, or a character quality you admire, etc. Choose a time to deliver your appreciation when you have his or her full attention, eye to eye. Say something like, "I've noticed that….," or "I really like …," or "I appreciate…" (act or attitude,) Remember that if you follow with a comment beginning with "But…," the value of the appreciation goes from being a positive to a definite negative. No "buts" allowed!

Add, "I want to make sure you really receive the truth of my words, so would you please repeat back to me what you heard me say?" And whether or not they repeat back, thank them.

A wonderful goal would be to make this a daily occurrence from you to everyone in your household, indefinitely. After maintaining this practice of appreciation for a month or more, you may find that appreciations are coming your way more frequently, as well.

LEARN EACH OTHER'S LOVE LANGUAGE

One of the first exercises I give couples I coach is to take the Love Languages Quiz at www.5lovelanguages.com Each of us has one primary and perhaps a secondary way that that we internalize the feeling of being loved. This is true for children as well as your partner. The five languages identified by Gary Chapman after years of counseling couples are *words of affirmation, receiving gifts, acts of service, physical touch and quality time.*

We all tend to give love in the language in which we feel the most loved. Rarely, however, do two partners both have the same love language. So, you may be expressing your love by *words of affirmation* (appreciation, praise, acknowledgement) but your partner is longing for some *quality time* with you.

When I discovered that Jim's primary love language was *words of affirmation,* I felt lost. As I shared above, I'd never heard *words of affirmation* growing up. It was not only hard for me to receive compliments, but I felt uncomfortable giving appreciations or compliments. I literally had to rehearse the words/sentences to say in order to express *words of affirmation* to Jim. After a few months of practice, however, the words began to come more naturally. I couldn't help but see the glow that came to Jim's face when he heard words of my genuine appreciation or acknowledgment. His positive responses encouraged me to keep it up!

A few years after learning to give Jim words of affirmation, my adult son who was an exemplary kid who pretty much steered himself successfully into adulthood while Jim and I navigated the really bad years of our marriage, confronted me with this question, "Mom, why didn't you ever acknowledge how good I was? I never heard you brag about me or share with me any appreciation for how easy I was for you during those years."

I felt his true words like a knife in my heart. I had been learning to give *words of affirmation* to Jim, but neglected to apply that skill to my son! Since that time, we never have a conversation or visit of any kind without me being generous with my words of appreciation or praise for at least one of the many fine character qualities he embodies or acknowledgment of some kindness he's done for me or someone else.

Now the *habit* of appreciation or acknowledgement has generalized to every relationship in my life...even to strangers I meet who are thoughtful or demonstrate some quality I admire.

KINDNESS

In a wonderful article by Emily Esfahani Smith in the Atlantic Monthly online magazine, June 12, 2014, she distills a great deal of marriage research by John Gottman into the importance of kindness in a happy marriage. She writes, *"There are many reasons why relationships fail, but if you look at what drives the deterioration of many relationships, it's often a breakdown of kindness.* As the normal stresses of a life together pile up—with children, career, friend, in-laws, and other distractions crowding out the time for romance and intimacy—couples may put less effort into their relationship and let the petty grievances they hold against one another tear them apart. In most marriages, levels of satisfaction drop dramatically within the first few years together. But among couples who not only endure, but live happily together for years and years, *the spirit of kindness and generosity guides them forward."* (Italics mine.)

She goes on to add, "We've all heard that partners should be there for each other when the going gets rough. But research shows that being there for each other when things go *right* is actually more important for relationship quality. How someone responds to a partner's *good news* can have dramatic consequences for the relationship. It's been found that, in general, couples responded to each other's good news in four different ways..."

I'll give you the bottom line of the research: The way that had the most positive long-term effect on the relationship was when a partner consistently responded positively and enthusiastically about *any good news* reported by his or her spouse...somewhat like a *cheerleader*. And wouldn't life be more fun if we all had a personal cheerleader? Someone we could count on to be in our corner? As well as someone we could count on to be kind?

KINDNESS EXERCISE

Kindness can take many forms: Forgiveness for a slight or lapse like being late, or forgetting the milk, a shoulder rub, or cuddling on the coach when your loved one has had a hard day. Kindness can be surrendering the remote control, or fixing a favorite meal or dessert. It might be picking up take-out for dinner when you know your partner is tired or stressed...or stopping to pick up her favorite candy bar, or hiding a package of his favorite flavor of gum where he'll find it unexpectedly.

DATING

Often one of the first relationship-sustaining behaviors that disappears in the chaos of a new stepfamily is the practice of dating. And yet, continuing to date regularly is one of the most dependable practices that enable a couple to survive, and even thrive, in the midst of multiple stresses and daily demands. Regularly can be once a week (preferred), twice monthly or monthly. But, because it's so easy to let this practice fade into the background, I recommend that you put your dates on the calendar, just like you would any other important appointment.

Even for dating, however, there must be a rule. To preserve its positive contribution to the marriage, fun dates must be protected from conflict. Topics likely to trigger upsets are to be avoided. My recommendation to couples I coach is to have two types of dates: 1) Skilled Discussion Dates and 2) Fun, Romantic Dates…and never let them overlap. If a touchy subject comes up during a Fun Date, immediately make a separate date for a Skilled Discussion about that topic, and resume your enjoyment of each other.

These dates do not have to be expensive or complicated. The goal is just to do something together that you both enjoy. Here are some suggestions: See a matinee' in the theater or from your own sofa; Hold hands while taking a walk or share a cup of coffee; Set aside a time each day to talk about the day and really listen to each other; Have breakfast, lunch, or dinner together without TV or interruptions; Agree on a time each day when you pray together; Make a point to greet each other when you come home and exchange kind words when you are parting; Walk or exercise together; Celebrate any milestone in your relationship; Set aside a time to give each other a massage; Build a table, refinish a bookcase, paint a room, plant a garden; Take turns attending an event that pleases your partner, such as a ball game, or home and garden show.

> **Nancy:** Many of my fondest memories of my years with Jim are the weekly dates he insisted that we have. After sending the kids off to school or a sitter, we'd go out to breakfast. If we had things to talk about, we enjoyed talking. If not, he'd do his crossword puzzle and I'd read my novel. We'd often go from there to a movie or to a table in the park where we played table games. Occasionally Jim would plan a mystery date for me that would take all day. One time he took me to a unique plant nursery. Another time he let take as long as I wanted to wander through a quilting supply store. These were both gifts of love as he hated shopping. (He was happy to wait in the car with the newspaper or a crossword puzzle!)
>
> Once he told me to bring a nice change of clothes. We attended a Hollywood musical that night…a show I'd expressed an interest in. After he died, I found a file folder where he'd collected ideas for future mystery dates that he thought I'd enjoy. These mystery dates were spontaneous…perhaps happening only every six months or so. Whether the events he planned really pleased me or were a bit blah, the fact that he'd made the effort to plan and execute a date that was designed to please only me, made me feel so loved, so treasured.
>
> And I, also, planned mystery dates for him with activities like going to an Angels baseball game, giving him a new crossword puzzle book by his favorite creator, or dining at his favorite barbeque restaurant.
>
> Our regular dates in addition to these mystery dates, were one of the practices that helped us survive the difficult years, and later, sustained the pleasure of our love during the years that we had left together.

DATING EXERCISE:

Open a file folder or a list in your phone or computer where you collect ideas for dates that would please your partner. Initiate a Discussion with your partner about planning regular dates. How often is feasible? How much time can you plan on? What do you both like to do? Who will arrange for a sitter for the children? Mark your dates on your calendars a year in advance. These dates are important and can only be adjusted, not deleted from your calendars.

Do you only have an hour? Go to the nearest Starbucks for a coffee break and chat. Or take a walk together through a nearby park.

NOTE: Dates are only marriage dates when it is the two of you alone. No children, no friends. Friends make it a social date. Children make it a family date.

Clients Richard and Katie were getting dressed for a night out. One of their children asked, "Are you going on a date? Together? Just the two of you?" The child then smiled... It adds to a child's sense of security to see his parent and step-parent getting ready for a date. (This couple had a history of heavy conflict. They were working hard to practice new skills to resolve their differences and stabilize their marriage. The children had been living with the scary awareness that their world was in danger of collapsing...again.)

KEEP AGREEMENTS

A critical part of building and maintaining trust is keeping agreements. Many step-couples, as well as their child or children, come from relationships where commitments or promises were not kept, so they are highly sensitized to issues of trust.

Nancy: Jim and I wanted so much to co-parent his young son, Jimmy. Over and over again we would work out, and agree on, a rule and consequences if Jimmy didn't follow through. My memory is no doubt imperfect, but it seemed at the time that Jim always had a reason to not enforce the consequences, or was mad at me for enforcing them in his absence. Over time, I lost confidence in his word...believing that I couldn't trust him. That loss of trust coincided for me in loss of respect for Jim.

In other chapters you'll hear about the parenting solution that helped us step out of that downward spiral of distrust. But a huge part of the recovery of our marriage was when Jim realized he must think through any of my suggestions carefully, and *only agree if he was sure he would follow through*. I would far rather he said, "No" to my proposal up front, than say, "Yes" and not back up his word with his behavior. By making this change, (and others) Jim regained my trust, *and* my respect.

COMMITMENT: The Grand Agreement

Some of my clients who have experienced great distress in a previous relationship or gone through a horrendous break-up cringe at the thought of completely, fully committing themselves to the present marriage. The additional challenges and stresses in a stepfamily that often require great strides in personal growth and simple endurance make the option of leaving this mess look even more enticing.

Mentally giving yourself an "out" if things get too bad makes even more sense if your partner isn't doing this stepfamily work the way that you want him/her to do it.

There are times, rarely, when getting out (and taking your child out) of an abusive relationship is the only sane option. To be clear, I'm not talking about staying in a relationship that is physically or sexually abusive to you or your child.

But, when you dream of leaving because this "stepfamily stuff" is just too hard, a back door is opened where your energy leaks out, rather than all of your energy being applied to implementing strategies that will eventually create a marriage and family that is strong and loving.

"Closing the Back Door" is the title of the final chapter in **How to Stay Married & Love It!** This marriage, this family need you all in…committed to learning and using the skills and strategies that will bring security, peace and lasting love to you, your partner and your child.

The eight-year old son of a man I was coaching who was preparing to remarry, said to his dad, **"This time, Dad, when you make a promise, I want you to keep it."** For this boy, the dissolution of his parents' marriage was interpreted as a betrayal of trust.

Author and marriage advocate, Gary Chapman says, "There are no problems that cannot be solved. There are only persons unwilling to solve them."

You may need to take regular mini-breaks…like two hours wandering through a mall by yourself. Or, a golf game with the guys. Or, three hours to read a great novel at your favorite park or beach. Or, a spa day with a girlfriend. You get the idea. Yes, take time to refresh yourself. You deserve it! And you need it! But closing the back door means you never, ever threaten to leave or make any reference to giving up on this marriage, this family. The "D" word (divorce) is forbidden.

"Commitment involves a *decision* to work with the fears and rigid patterns that arise in a relationship. Conscious commitment is *to being* together, not just staying together." John Welwood, Ph.D. in **Journey of the Heart.**

It is difficult to create "...a happy second marriage without also creating a workable stepfamily" (Hetherington & Kelly, 2002, p. 179.) "And a workable stepfamily is *impossible to* create without a strong, loving marriage!" (Nancy Landrum)

Stumbling Blocks to Building a Strong and Loving Marriage:[1]
____ Assuming our marriage will survive the stresses because we "love each other."
____ Letting the demands of stepfamily life crowd out the needs of the marriage.____ Taking my frustrations with a child out on my spouse (or vice versa).
____ Letting more than 24 hours go by without a respectful discussion when there is an upset.
____ Breaking our agreements with each other.
____ Developing a "special" relationship with a child to the exclusion of my spouse.
____ Keeping secrets from my spouse or encouraging a child to keep secrets.
____ Allowing the children to play us against each other.
____ Expecting this undertaking to be easy.
____ Expecting this family to work like the American ideal of a "first" or nuclear family.
____ Forgetting why we love each other!

Building Blocks to Building a Strong and Loving Marriage:
____ Dating regularly.
____ Finding dependable child care. (Do not leave younger children with older step-siblings until you're sure a caring bond has developed.)
____ Attending a marriage enrichment event at least once per year.
____ Practicing respectful discussions and problem solving with any issue.
____ Using honest and caring communication skills.
____ When too upset to use good skills, choosing conflict management strategies. (Time out! Venting!)
____ Finding a stepfamily support group in our community.
____ Finding and doing activities together that we both enjoy.
____ Allowing each other "alone" or "other friends" times when needed.
____ Keeping my agreements.
____ Supporting and enforcing the agreed upon house rules.
____ Making sure my emotional connections to a former spouse are healed.
____ Understanding my spouse's need to have alone time with his/her bio-child.
____ Remembering the good in each other.
____ Checking out our expectations against the research. Are they realistic?
____ Giving parenting advice to each other only when asked.
____ Making time and space for my spouse's needs.

---

[1]The Stumbling Blocks and Building Blocks lists throughout this book are not intended as rigid rules but were compiled from research outcomes verifying what elements frequently contribute to stepfamily failure and success. First extracted from multiple research reports by Nancy Landrum and published in *Mastering the Mysteries of Stepfamilies*, by Relationship Press, 2009.

SUMMARY

There are many habits that nurture a strong and loving marriage...or any other relationship. Don't be so overwhelmed that you neglect to pick one and begin!

BUILDING TASKS: Add Nurturing Behaviors and Activities

What is your marriage lacking? Fun? Private time? Skilled Discussions to find workable solutions? Use the Stumbling Blocks list to note the things that need attention. Use the Building Blocks list to celebrate what you're doing well...and keep doing those things! Agree on regular dates and put them on your calendars months in advance. These are sacred times for your marriage! Make giving appreciations a daily habit. Take the **Love Languages** quiz online and then be sure to frequently deliver love to your spouse in the language that means the most to him or her. And cultivate frequent kind acts to everyone in your household.

COMING UP...

Learn how to parent in ways that support a strong and loving marriage.

CHAPTER SIX: Parenting to Support the Marriage

Being a parent brings out the most protective and vulnerable feelings. This being that we brought into the world begins as totally dependent on us for every need. The main task of parenting is to give this child the safety, support, and encouragement in order to reach independence.

There are several styles of parenting. I once read that it isn't being permissive or strict that determines a healthy outcome for a child, but whether the parents are in agreement and consistent.

Some step-couples are able to move seamlessly into a parenting or co-parenting style that works for them and the child.

But for many, this is the first and most potent issue that raises its ugly head soon after the whole family is under one roof. As you've heard before, this was true for Jim and me. It was also true for Ted, Julie, Kip and Wendy.

TED AND JULIE

>**Julie:** Ted is very structured in the way he parents. I am far more relaxed. Ted's family told him to leave me. When he refused, they broke off all contact with us. We were spiraling downward. Very little could be discussed. We had fights in front of the kids, about the kids. We had no dates, no time for us. Everything had become a competition. My kids had had no contact with their adoptive or biological father since 2005. I wanted Ted to be a loving father-figure to them, but he was so strict. We were constantly criticizing each other's parenting decisions.

>**Ted:** (After Nancy listened) to each of us describe what was happening from our respective points of view, she asked if we were ready to take steps for immediate relief. We would have done anything at that point! We loved each other and were heart-broken that we couldn't seem to make our marriage work. Without doing something differently, we were teetering on the brink of another separation.

>**Julie:** She described the guideline recommended for stepfamilies who have conflicts over parenting. We would go back to single parenting our respective children. The step-parent would not comment or criticize the bio-parent's children or parenting methods. We would agree on a few simple house rules[2] by which everyone in the family would abide.

>It hit me hard. When I told Nancy that I just wanted a man who would love my children, she replied, "It's too late to have a nuclear family. That time is gone. You're in a stepfamily now and most stepfamilies only succeed by functioning with different strategies than first families.

---
[2] The House Rules instructions are at the end of this chapter.

Ted: But we were so desperate we'd do anything to stop the fights, so we agreed. No commenting or criticizing of each other's children or parenting decisions. We'd focus on rebuilding relationships with our own children.

Julie: Over the next few days it was like a magic pill had been dropped into our home. The fighting immediately stopped! The calm was like a breath of fresh, cleansing air after being in a smoke-filled room! But I also grieved the loss of my first-family dream. I grieved the loss of a loving father for my children. I cried off and on for two weeks.

(But then) the love we knew was buried under everything all along returned in force. We've gone on romantic dates! We have rediscovered why we've been friends through all of these years. The kids have calmed down. The whole family had been divided in half, but now relationships between the kids are healing. There is laughter in our house again!

It felt like the solution to change back to single-parenting was a bomb that dropped in the middle of our family. Everything flew in all directions. Our expectations had been so unrealistic. Now we know that stepfamilies often require thinking outside the nuclear family box. We're slowly figuring out how to put our family back together in ways that work for us and our children.

Ted: Right after the class we thought everything was fixed, but in the months since then we've realized that a lot of damage was done during the chaotic years. Now we are taking things one step at a time. As we and the children feel more secure, layers of issues are surfacing that require us to continue using our skills and stepfamily guidelines. We're doing a better job of listening to our children.

Now that we're not busy being defensive with each other about our parenting, we're becoming more attentive to the needs of our own children. We're more realistic about the fact that our stepfamily issues will continue to be a challenge, probably for the rest of our lives. Our children will continue to need our love and support as they move into adulthood with the wounds from their childhoods. We hope that they will follow our lead by learning these skills to make their first and only marriage succeed. We pray that they will stop the legacy of divorce with all its pain and chaos that Julie and I have handed them.

Julie: The great news is that the kids are living with a model of a healthy marriage for the first time in their lives! Ted and I are absolutely sure now that we will stay together and love each other until parted by death! It feels indescribably safe to have that security!

My advice given to Ted and Julie the first time we met together came straight from Jim's and my personal experience and from the research I studied later. When I "resigned" as Jimmy's mom and Jim resumed parenting him alone, we thought we were the worst failures in the world! It was only several years later that we learned that when hundreds of stepfamilies were studied to determine the elements that enabled some to succeed and others to fail, each parenting their own children...separately...was one of the main characteristics of stepfamilies that functioned well.

KIP AND WENDY: (I asked what they experienced as their biggest challenge.)

Wendy: Parenting, definitely! We've raised our children differently. We have different personality types and temperaments. To try to "blend" our kids and our styles was not practical. Our kids were not toddlers. Neither of us could change our styles of discipline. We came to the conclusion through counseling and communication classes that we both have to be OK doing it the way we've done it and not trying to "blend" it or have a one-system program for everyone. We had to make sure that the kids knew that it wasn't going to be equal for all. Although we've tried to make *some* things uniform, (House Rules) discipline and the way we handle conflict is definitely different for each of us.

Kip: I'm a lot more easy-going with my kids. Wendy is more straight-forward…"This is the way it's going to be." Initially Wendy would tell me what she thought I should do with my son who has lived with us the most. Because I wanted to please Wendy, I'd go to Greg and say, "It's going to be this way." He'd be shocked because it was so different than I would normally have handled it. Eventually he'd say, "Dad, I know you only said that because you're trying to please Wendy." One other time he made the comment, "Dad, I don't know if you know this or not, but Wendy is NOT my mom!" By that point, we'd learned enough that I said to him, "You're absolutely right! She's not your mom! She'll never be your mom. You have a mom who loves you. I hope you'll eventually become good friends with Wendy. But in the meantime, she's my wife."

Wendy: Kip's strength is grace. He's able to look past things that I would find offensive. I'm more structured, disciplined. I expect them to follow the rules and be obedient. You might even say I'm more militant. Part of it was survival. My kids' dad was not as involved as I wished he was. When Kip and I got together he was very passive about discipline. I came on strong in the beginning to try to compensate. (Nancy: This is a common attempt in stepfamilies that only results in each parent becoming more attached to his/her method of parenting.) Over time I observed that there's strength in his grace and he's seen that there are areas where he needs to step up and be more firm on certain issues. We've worked out a balance. But most importantly, we each discipline our own children. When we need to agree because it's a whole-family issue or it affects other family members, understanding our differences helps us to reach an agreement that suits us both.

Kip: There's times when Wendy has come to me and said, "If you make this decision about Greg, I'm concerned about how it's going to affect my kids. For instance, I've told them they can't go see that movie." So sometimes I've gone to Greg and said, "I don't feel comfortable with you going to that movie." He'll fight it, but I make the decision for the benefit of everyone. Our kids are close to the same age. It doesn't always work that way, but we try, as much as possible, to be considerate of how our decisions affect the other's kids.

Wendy: (In working together on a joint decision) the deciding factor for me is whether our difference is just a preference…like whether or not the beds are made every day. The other—like the movie—is a moral or values issue. A decision about the movie is based on "Is it going to influence them negatively?" That's a values issue. Making the bed or not can be a lesson about discipline or housekeeping but it's not going to determine their path in life.

Nancy: Juggling these differences in parenting styles may sound very unwieldy...awkward...impossible, even. But Elizabeth Einstein, author of the great stepfamily program called Active Parenting for Stepfamilies disagrees. She states, "Children can cope with two different homes and sets of rules if they don't have to choose which is best."

In Kip and Wendy's home, the kids were living with two different sets of rules (about some things) while under the same roof. How do they manage?

> **Wendy**: I think there are a lot of couples out there who think that there must to be only one way to handle all the kids. *One* way can be that there are *two* ways under the same roof. *We make it work because we don't judge each other's methods of handling our respective children and we work together on the issues that affect everyone.* Our kids, even the ones with the same biology, have different personalities and require different things. It's OK to have different systems.

Wendy explained to me that when one of her kids complained to her, "Kip's kids get to .... Why can't I?" Wendy answered, "It's Kip's job to do the best parenting he can for his children and it's my job to make the best decisions I can for my children. You are my child, and I believe that it's best if you..."

The fact that they never criticized each other's parenting, but supported each other's parenting decisions, soon eliminated the complaints.

> **Kip:** If we hadn't gone through the process we did before the wedding—if we were still trying to handle things the way we were before all the classes and counseling—we would already be divorced, or at the least, be miserable! In the beginning when Wendy's daughters would come to me to ask about something they wanted, I answered, "Ask your mom. She makes the decisions about you." This nipped in the bud any tendency the kids had to play us against each other.

Most of the agony that Jim and I experienced could have been avoided if we had known the one primary principle that works for most stepfamilies. It is the concept of **BIOLOGICALLY DRIVEN PARENTING.** We eventually learned that our original expectation that I would fully be Jimmy's parent, was unreasonable. It very, very rarely works.

PARENTING THAT WORKS

Biologically Driven Parenting is promoted by the Stepfamily Association of America as well as a growing number of experts on stepfamily dynamics. It is characterized by these practices:

- The biological parent is always the primary parent and always the source of any discipline.
- The bio-parent and the step-parent discuss the parenting plans in private, perhaps even take a parenting class together. They agree on specific house rules and consequences of misbehavior. Ideally both agree, but the final decision is always the bio-parent's. House rules are written down for the benefit of adults and child/ren.
- The bio-parent takes the lead in dealing with the child. The step-parent backs up the bio-parent so the child cannot pit them against each other.
- The bio-parent follows through consistently with the plans agreed upon, first of all for the benefit of the child, but also so that the step-parent is not placed in the intolerable position of being an adult, helplessly at the mercy of a misbehaving child.

- The step-parent backs up the written rules as a messenger, not the source of the discipline. Such as, "Your Mom/Dad said you are to..."
- Lapses of discipline or annoying infractions of house rules are issues that are settled first between the partners, and then between the biological parent and child.
- The step-parent curbs the desire to control, scold, or discipline the step-child.
- The step-parent only offers feedback to the bio-parent about the step-child with permission and only with respectful communication. It's a little like avoiding a land-mine because the bio-parent is deeply, and instinctively protective of the child if that child is attacked or his/her parenting skills are attacked.

These guidelines are challenging to follow. These easily reactive dynamics are the major reason why creating a stable, loving stepfamily is so difficult. It requires putting the marriage and the welfare of the children ahead of our personal preferences. One stepfather reported to me,

"I began to feel like a permanent assistant coach. I was there on the sidelines, there at halftime, but ultimately, I made none of the decisions. I had to accept that they weren't my children...I had to focus on stewardship and service, not ownership. I also had to accept that I didn't have a fan club. The kids would never run to greet me with the words, 'Daddy's here!'"

THE ULTIMATE ADVANTAGES OF BIO-DRIVEN PARENTING FOR THE STEP-PARENT

Nancy: I thought my heart would break when I relinquished my role as a traditional mom to Jimmy. The change in dynamic had almost instantaneous benefits, however:
- I no longer had the responsibility of trying to figure out what was best for Jimmy. That was now entirely up to Jim.
- My only responsibility was to work with Jim when decisions concerning Jimmy directly affected me.
- An essential part of our agreement was that I would not even offer advice or suggestions unless Jim asked for them.
- It wasn't long before I began to feel relieved that the responsibility was no longer mine.
- A huge source of conflict was eliminated between Jim and me.
- The problems Jimmy was having could no longer be blamed on me.
- Without the struggles being focused on me, and what I was doing to cause problems with Jimmy, Jim soon realized that Jimmy had some needs that were not being met by his parenting practices. He was eager to get help. He began implementing an active parenting plan that provided far more healthy guidance for Jimmy.

It took a while for us to regain our trust in each other . . . trust that we would each honor the new "rules" to which we had agreed. There were slips, but overall, we experienced an instant, gigantic leap forward in the regaining of our love.

SUMMARY
There *is* hope for stepfamilies. Strategies that enable a stepfamily to succeed are different than in a biological or nuclear family. Accepting and co-operating with that truth minimizes our struggles. There will be more about parenting and step-parenting in future chapters, but the biologically driven parenting concept is in

support of a successful marriage *and more well-adjusted children*. Although the guidelines for implementing this process are clear, *they only become clear to you* as you work them out between you and your partner.

BUILDING TASKS:

It takes multiple times of clarifying your priorities to navigate through the issues that get triggered by stepfamily dynamics and strategies. Are you willing to put the welfare of your marriage ahead of your ideas of how a stepchild *should* be parented? Are you, the bio-parent willing to assume full responsibility for the welfare of your child? And do your best to work with the child's other bio-parent for the benefit of the child?

The **House Rules Exercise** at the end of this chapter is a great antidote for the powerlessness that sometimes swamps a stepparent. There is more about parenting and step-parenting in later chapters.

COMING UP...

How to you handle finances? Separate accounts? Joint? Other differences in the handling of money in regard to your children?

Optional (but Highly Recommended) Exercise: The Stepfamily-Five House Rules

Purpose: To establish a few basic rules the apply to everyone in the family. These rules are particularly important so the step-parent has some say in what happens in a home that he/she shares. In the case where each adult has children in the home, it's also essential for the children to see that some rules apply to everyone, no exceptions. With the House Rules, both adults have equal right to enforce the consequences if broken. It will be very helpful to you to watch the brief video testimony of how beneficial the House Rules were to Sherman and Alexa. The adults made the rules, but the kids got to choose the consequences. Very interesting! http://nancylandrum.com/stepping-twogether

Directions: Print out two copies of the House Rules suggestions. Each partner check off the five rules (or certainly less than ten) that are your "must have" or "can't possibly live without" conditions for being reasonably comfortable in your home. Other rules you may enforce with your own child if they are important to you, but those rules are not imposed on the whole family.

His: Hers:

___   ___   We make major decisions as a family: Family Meetings (Watch James and Kim talk about Family Meetings: http://nancylandrum.com/stepping-twogether)

___   ___   Everyone home for a sit-down dinner.

___   ___   Chores done before recreational activities on weekends.

___   ___   Everyone observes the "knock and wait for permission to enter" rule.

___ ___ Modest dress outside your bedroom.
___ ___ Monday (or some other night) is dinner and game night.
___ ___ No cursing or foul language.
___ ___ Everyone says "please" and "thank you."
___ ___ No "borrowing" (clothes, jewelry, equipment, money) without permission.
___ ___ No children in the Master Bedroom.
___ ___ No talking back.
___ ___ No hitting.
___ ___ No TV until homework finished.
___ ___ TV watching and video games limited to ___ minutes or hours/day.
___ ___ Everyone over 12 years old or older does their own laundry.
___ ___ Everyone busses their own dirty dishes.
___ ___ Bed made every day.
___ ___ Towels always hung up after a bath.
___ ___ Everyone pitches in for Saturday chores.
___ ___ Chew with your mouth closed.
___ ___ No food in the living room.
___ ___ Everyone busses their own dishes. No dishes left in the sink.
___ ___ No fussing about bedtime.
___ ___ Curfews obeyed.
___ ___ Everyone in church once/week.
___ ___ ___minute limit on phone calls.
___ ___ School attendance. Homework done by ___.
___ ___ Once/day baths.

Others vitally important to you:

___ ___ _____
___ ___ _____
___ ___ _____
___ ___ _____
___ ___ _____

Step 1. Do you have rules that over-lap? Are they very different? Have a Skilled Dialogue about these options until you can pare the list down to under ten rules that will be expected of every family member including yourselves. This may take several sessions! The effort will be worth it in reducing conflict and confusion.

Step 2. Circle or highlight the rules you both agree on for the Stepfamily Five.

Step 3. Decide on the consequences for violation of each of the rules. (The consequences may be different for each child depending on what motivates each child, their age, or the consequences may be the same for all. It's up to you! Or take your cue from Alexa and Sherman and ask the kids to choose the consequences.)

Step 4. Have a family meeting to jointly present the House Rules to the children. Decide who will post the rules and consequences in a place where everyone in the family will see them regularly. (Perhaps the frig, like Sherman and Alexa.)

Step 5. Build trust and reduce conflict by keeping your agreements: enforce rules and consequences for your child.

Step 6. If your spouse fails to enforce the rules with his/her child, ask for a Skilled Discussion. Share your feelings. Renegotiate or recommit to the rules. These rules are not just for the children, but to support a happy marriage.

She: Are there additional things that you will expect of your child, but is up to your spouse to decide on for his child?

_____

How I will handle it when my child complains that she/he doesn't have to do that!

_____

He: Are there additional things that you will expect of your child, but is up to your spouse to decide on for his/her child?

_____

How I will handle it when my child complains that she/he doesn't have to do that!

_____

Note: Mary Ortwein MSW, who contributed significantly to this text, counseled a step-mom who had **ninety-five** written rules that her step-children were supposed to obey. Every night at bedtime she went over the rules that each had broken. Can you imagine the resentment being cultivated in their hearts by this alpha step-mom? And the anger toward their father for neglecting to protect them from this emotional abuse?

Having a few simple, most essential House Rules for everyone with predictable, knowable consequences makes sharing a home so much simpler for both adults and children. The challenge for the adults is consistently enforcing the rules…always the drawback of any rule! But the more consistent the enforcement, the easier the home life becomes. Please do watch Sherman and Alexa's testimony about the value of House Rules: www.nancylandrum.com/stepping-twogether

Stumbling Blocks to Managing House Rules:

___ Insisting that my rules are the best or must be the only rules for everyone.
___ Displaying judgment about my spouse's "too strict" or "too lenient" rules.
___ Being condescending because my rules for my children are "better" than my partner's.
___ Criticizing or belittling my partner's rules to my children or step-children
___ Making too many House Rules.

Building Blocks for Managing House Rules

___ Consistently enforcing the House Rules with my children.
___ Accepting that we may have different values or perspectives about rules for children.
___ Expecting my child to live by the guidelines I believe are best for him/her.
___ Enforcing rules with my step-child only when my spouse is not present and I have permission.
___ Keeping House Rules as simple and basic as possible.

CHAPTER SEVEN: Money Management That Supports the Marriage

I confess. I have no magic answers about financial management. The biggest problem Jim and I had with money was that we were both marginal money managers and both loved to spend. Our patterns led us into some very poor decisions and some very lean years.

What we did have, though, by the time the lean years hit, were the communication skills that prevented the financial stress from damaging our relationship. We didn't blame each other. We didn't fight. We just dug in and learned some budgeting skills and made some tough decisions that eventually allowed us to emerge intact.

So, let's hear from other members of our cast...

CHARLES AND CAROLE

Carole: At one time finances were a big challenge. The best take-away I can offer is that no matter how much you talk about something in detail before you marry, it's not enough. The devil's in the details! We talked about a lot of things when we were engaged. We agreed to support children through the earning of their Bachelor's Degrees. When the oldest one went to college, Charles said he would make it happen no matter where they wanted to go. My idea was to give them a price range and they could go anywhere within that price range. I didn't want them to apply to a $60K/year college and tell them we would work it out! I was uncomfortable with an unlimited commitment to tuition. And each application costs $200! I wanted to limit the number of apps they sent in!

Charles: Because of these "discussions" it's easy to give up and say they'll all pay for their own education! It's often easy to do the *easy-wrong* instead of the *hard-right*. But we didn't give up. We figured it out. Carole made some recommendations and I accepted half of them, but we worked it out.

KIP AND WENDY

Wendy: I don't know that (finances) was a BIG issue although we had different styles in that area, too. I had some insecurities about finances that came from my previous marriage and the way my Ex handled money. I was also the youngest of five girls raised by a single parent and grew up with very little. I am an independent woman. Even though I didn't make a lot of money I wanted to spend it *my* way.

Although we agreed that full disclosure was important before we got married, it took a while for me to trust Kip. We agreed that we would each clean up any bad credit or debt before we got married so that we could get married debt-free. We each took responsibility for cleaning up our own stuff. We agreed to *not* go into debt for a wedding. We started off with very little income and no home—no major assets. We were in agreement about that part of our finances, although there were definitely some things we had to overcome. They weren't major. Along the way we came together on the way things are handled.

Kip: A year ago we bought our first home together and recently had a huge house-warming party. It was quite a celebration of how far we've come together! Full disclosure was very important to Wendy but also for me. I was shocked a couple of times when I bought something for her and she was upset about it because I didn't get her OK to spend the money! I thought, "I bought this for you and you're upset?"

Wendy: I'd have a *huge* emotional response.

Kip: But we worked through those times. We both agreed that it is critical for us to be wide-open about all financial decisions.

Wendy: Over time we've done what we said we were going to do and that's built trust between us. It's reduced some of the excessive emotional reaction from me.

Kip: That's the other good thing about waiting the extra year. By making sure we were both completely out of debt and saving money for our wedding, we eliminated a huge potential source of conflict.

Wendy: We have two children who have asked us to co-sign a loan and another who's asked for a temporary loan saying, "I'll pay you back in two weeks." We have children with different needs. We took time to talk about it and came back with decisions that are not partial to one side of the family or the other. Our decision has been, "We won't co-sign with you but we'll gift you a certain amount."

TED AND JULIE

Ted and Julie shared with me that they had conflicts over differing policies regarding the money spent on their respective children. In order to avoid the conflicts, Julie would hide purchases she made for her children that were contrary to their marriage agreements. Some time after learning the Communication and Problem-Solving Skills in class, Julie sent this email to me:

"I had to share this with you! Ted and I had a skilled Problem-Solving Discussion about our kids and money spent on them. It has been a touchy subject! But this time was so awesome! We shared, listened and went deep (becoming more and more vulnerable and truthful) and understood each other and *stayed in respectful skills the whole time!* We couldn't finish in one talk, but we are coming back later because we learned so much about each other. It is an amazing victory for us. We have accomplished what seemed impossible even three weeks ago!"

These are just a few of the money-driven sources of conflict for a step-couple. It seems that most of us are as defensive and protective of our financial dealings as we are about our children. As with all the other potential sources of stress, knowing and using good, respectful communication skills is essential for successfully coming to agreement.

It doesn't seem to matter whether or not you have joint or separate bank accounts, whether you share equally in the expenses of your stepfamily house or divvy them up proportional to your respective incomes. It doesn't matter who pays for what. What matters is:

1. You are both scrupulously truthful about your financial condition before and during your marriage.
2. You work out agreements that are satisfactory to both of you.
3. You keep your agreements with each other
    a. About money spent on each child.
    b. About household budgets.
    c. About saving for the future.
4. You agree on an amount above which you will not spend without the knowledge and approval of the other. That amount can be as little as $20 or as much as $500 depending on what is comfortable for both of you. This includes not taking on debt without agreement.

This concept has helped many of my clients... there are decisions that are appropriately up to the individual. Those decisions do not impact the health or safety of the relationship. I call those independent decisions. There are other decisions that must be decided jointly. Those are marriage decisions.

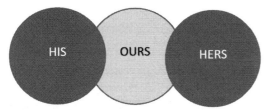

It's up to each couple to decide which decisions can be made independently and which need to be made jointly in order to protect the relationship.

A recent example:

Recent clients had a history of getting along great...until things build up and an explosion erupted that left both shaken and hurt. Now they are learning how to bring issues up in a Skilled Discussion so that they can be resolved in a way that suits them both.

A recent example they shared with me: Each December they throw a giant holiday party for friends and family, most of whom are not as comfortable financially as they are. Last year, without consulting him, she went completely overboard buying gifts for each person who would attend. They were thinly disguised as rewards for games played. He didn't realize the excess until he saw the type and value of each gift as it was received and opened.

He did not object so much to the amount of money spent, but on the likelihood that many of their friends and family members would be upset that they couldn't afford reciprocal gifts of like value. He was embarrassed.

In a Skilled Discussion, she agreed that she'd been excessive and didn't consider the emotional impact on him or their guests. When I drew the above diagram for them, they immediately understood the difference between independent and joint decisions. She apologized and agreed that big expenditures needed to be discussed and agreed upon jointly.

They have gone on to apply this concept to many of their other decisions to clarify and prevent future conflicts.

This concept can be applied to any area in any relationship. The lines drawn between independent decisions that are OK with both parties and marriage decisions that need to be made jointly will differ from couple to couple.

THE FUTURE

Another aspect that is difficult for some step-couples to address is the need for each to have a Will and if recommended, a Living Trust. Each partner may come to the relationship with different assets. You may wish a particular asset to be preserved for your birth child/ren. Other assets that are jointly purchased may be divided equally between step- and birth children. The most loving thing you can do for your partner and your joint family is to make those tough decisions ahead of time. Without plainly prescribed wishes, the law will decide who gets what after your death. It's a predictable set up for possible disagreements and fights that may tear apart the stepfamily you worked so hard to establish.

I've had the personal experience of being widowed twice. The first time, we were so young, we hadn't even considered the possibility of the impact of an early death. My first husband did not have a will. It took four years to finally settle his very modest estate.

When Jim died, many things were difficult, but the financial choices had been made years before and were put into practice with only one appointment with our attorney.

I strongly recommend having that tough conversation now, and drawing up the legal documents that reflect your desires. I also recommend that the plans be reviewed every five years at a minimum.

SUMMARY

Financial conditions and choices are the second most frequent cause of step-couple conflicts (following parenting.) It requires bravery and commitment to the ultimate success of the relationship to tackle tough conversations about money, both how it is handled now and how it will be handled should one of you die before the other.

Note: If you agree on the goal of reducing or eliminating your debt, Jim and I found this little book helpful and easy to follow, **How to Get Out of Debt and Live Prosperously** by Jerrold Mundis. Based on the Proven Principles and Techniques of Debtors Anonymous.

BUILDING TASK

Tackle the tough conversations about money. Decide on a money management plan that you both are comfortable supporting. Budget some of your money for individual purchases, and definitely have dates as a budget item! Do the "hard, right thing" as Charles advises, and draw up wills. You can do simple inexpensive versions from LegalZoom.com or if your assets are more complicated, see an attorney. Check this biggie off of your list of loving choices for each other and your children. Don't make the mistake of assuming the other will know what you want, or will do what is best for your children.

COMING UP...

How do you conduct dealings with your Ex? Does the relationship with your Ex support the health of your current marriage?

CHAPTER EIGHT: The Ex...and Others

Healthy Boundaries are needed in any relationship, but vitally important for a step-couple. The failure of a previous relationship often leaves wounds and insecurities that need to be navigated in order for the new relationship to thrive.

I'll address your relationship with a difficult Ex in a later chapter, but right now, your relationship with an Ex and how it affects your current relationship is what is covered in this chapter.

This was a second marriage for Rich and Katie. Her father had been unfaithful to her mother multiple times. Her first husband had been unfaithful. The threat of infidelity was a huge issue for Katie. She didn't like Rich's close friendship with Mary. Even though Rich insisted the relationship had never been sexual, Katie demanded that the severing of this friendship was a prerequisite to their marriage. Rich explained to Mary, and left the friendship. (With help, there may have been other solutions to this issue.)

Mary sold organic vegetables at a local farmers' market. Rich ran into her while also there selling his organic vegetables. In their casual chat, he told her where his farmland was located. Mary came by to see his operation, unannounced, uninvited. Katie happened to drop by to see Rich while Mary was still looking around. The fuse was lit. Katie exploded with fury and a fusillade of accusations. She immediately said she wanted a divorce.

We all have unhealed wounds that sit like hidden land mines just below the surface. If or when our partner's behavior steps on the buried land mine, it explodes.

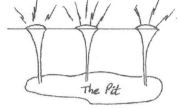

Former relationships, whether sexual or not, can be land mines in your new, fragile partnership. With social media such a huge part of our lives now, it's so easy to look up an old girlfriend, or say "Hi" to a high school sweetheart. It's dangerous territory and often puts extra pressure and stress on a step-couple who is already dealing with excessive stress.

If there are difficult issues whittling away at your step-couple relationship, it may feel harmless to connect with an old flame...to reach back to a relationship that, in the distance, looks safe and conflict free. "Just curious," you might say.

Commitment to doing all you can to support the health and security of your stepfamily means giving the gift of total transparency and honesty with your current partner. Gaye and Kathlyn Hendricks in their book *Conscious Loving* call this "telling the microscopic truth."

How this looks:

- No computer files or texts are password protected. Your partner has total access anytime he or she needs to use your phone.
- Or, you both know any passwords needed for your respective devices.

- You are both committed to being microscopically truthful answering any question with honesty and without defensiveness.
- And, you both agree to believe what your partner tells you.

The dangers are not just from previous romantic relationships. Sometimes a friend becomes your confidante about all things personal rather than cultivating an emotionally intimate relationship with your partner.

This does not mean that it's ok for either of you to become obsessively invasive, virtually stalking your partner, driven by your fears. It may mean that neither of you have other-sex friendships outside of your marriage. It simply means that you keep respectful boundaries in all relationships and especially when it means building the trust you both need in *this* relationship. It *always* means that you are both totally transparent about any contact with an other-sex person outside of your marriage. And you don't wait to be asked but volunteer information about any contact with an other-sex person...friend or business.

In regard to your Ex, you keep your interactions business like...deciding on schedules for the children, for instance. You do not pursue or encourage personal conversations regarding the problems he's having in his current romance, or your frustrations with stepfamily issues. Other than co-parenting your children, custody or child-support issues, your business with your Ex is finished.

This may be hard when your body remembers what it was like to be intimate...some of the good times. You may even find yourself aroused by his voice or her presence. Your body is simply reacting like Pavlov's dogs...to an old, pleasurable stimulus. Is it worth acting on when you have so much at stake? So much that is new and would be devastating to lose?

INFIDELTY: Is it possible to recover?

A few years ago, I was invited to attend an all-day training for therapists on how to help a couple recover from infidelity. Dave Carder, author of the book, **Torn Asunder**, was there to teach us how he had helped multiple couples either recover trust and commitment in their marriage, or be able to let the marriage go in peace. I decided to attend, knowing that someday one of my couples would need my help with this issue.

The following Tuesday Jack and Shirley called for an appointment. Over their twenty-two year marriage, he had been unfaithful three different times. The key here is that they both wanted to preserve their marriage, but also wanted to get past the pain of betrayal, the shame and the insecurity that pervaded their relationship.

I combined the exercises mapped out in the **Torn Asunder Workbook** with the communication skills I normally teach. Jack and Shirley were diligent in doing all of the reading and homework assignments. Together we explored the history of their relationship as well as flaws that contributed to the set-up for his affairs. There were no excuses. No defenses. Only information gathering and understanding growing about how they both contributed to this fissure in their marriage.

They learned and practiced new communication skills that helped them build a deep emotional connection that had really never been there before. They learned how to make marriage decisions together, rather than being two independent individuals that happened to cohabitate. They agreed on boundaries that they both kept.

Last year I received this email from Shirley: "We are happiest we have ever been. Our sex life is the best ever! We're so glad we did the hard work of dissecting the past, forgiving, and putting it behind us. We are committed to each other as long as we both are on this earth."

This wonderful example doesn't mean it is simple or easy to rebuild a relationship that has been torn apart by infidelity. It only means that when both parties want to save the marriage badly enough, it can be done!

BACK TO RICH AND KATIE

The day following the bomb exploding over the unplanned visit of Rich's former friend, they came to me, Katie still angry and ready to file for divorce. I quizzed Rich in depth and determined that he might have handled the situation a bit better, but that he was being truthful about not inviting Mary to visit his farm. In fact, as soon as she drove up, he asked her to leave. Katie arrived before Mary had a chance to get out of there.

I turned to Katie and practiced Listening to Understand as she unburdened her hurt and fear. Without taking the time to check out her assumptions, she had jumped to the conclusion that Rich had continued to be secretive about his relationship with Mary and that Mary's visit was at his invitation.

We dug deeper. Her father's infidelity to her mother and Katie's Ex's unfaithfulness to her left deeply buried landmines that exploded into rage when she found Mary at Rich's farm. After many tears, she saw that her buried wounds had provoked the explosion of violent rage and unproven beliefs. The threat to file for divorce was the predictable action she grabbed in her attempt to protect herself from further pain.

Before the session was over, she accepted Rich's apology for not making sure that Mary left the moment she arrived and she believed him when he assured her it was not a planned assignation. He forgave her for jumping to conclusions without allowing him to explain and for not believing him.

Now they are continuing their journey of putting into practice the skills they've learned using those skills to build a stronger "house" to hold their love. I heard through a mutual friend that they are still doing well!

ANOTHER COMMON ISSUE

Henry was still emotionally attached to his Ex. He felt guilty for whatever part he had played in the failure of their marriage. His current wife, Arletta, naturally resented the personal phone conversations that Henry still had with his Ex. In addition, he was paying his Ex almost twice the alimony that he was legally required to pay while he and Arletta were going further and further into debt.

Henry hasn't done the emotional work of *grieving* and truly *leaving* his first wife. The weight of his guilt and the pull of those emotional ties are threatening the health and wellbeing of his current marriage.

Boundaries are not just to keep yourself and others from inappropriate intimacy, but to surround your marriage with strong walls that protect it, allowing a safe environment in which to thrive.

EXTENDED FAMILY ISSUES

My late husband, Jim, (a pastor) performed many wedding ceremonies. It was very obvious if the parents of the bride or groom were divorced and still considered their power-plays to be more important than the quality of their child's wedding experience. The most obvious battle grounds were the order of being seated, who sat where, and who was included in which photo.

At one spectacular event, the families kept 300 guests waiting while they battled over whether or not the groom would take on the bride's last name rather than the more customary opposite. The mother of the bride eventually marched to the platform and announced the wedding was off, but everyone was welcome to come enjoy the food at the reception since they could not get a refund!

In stark contrast was the attitude and experience of Wendy at her step-son's wedding...

> **Wendy:** We traveled out of state for Kip's son's wedding. A large condo had been rented to house us. Kips Ex was also slated to stay in that condo. Although I had no doubts about Kip's love and loyalty toward me, it was hard to share the space—even the bathroom—with his Ex. I had to keep reminding myself that this event was not about me and my comfort. It was about giving Kip's son and his bride the best, most loving wedding environment possible. We did everything we could to give him that gift, but it was really hard!

The complexities of the extended family of steps is mind-boggling. In a first marriage, adjustments owing to differing family patterns and demands of in-laws may be difficult. In a stepfamily, the issues multiply exponentially. More and more often, the grandparents of the children have also divorced and remarried! It could be hard to find a piece of paper large enough to hold the family tree of some children.

CHARLES and CAROLE

> **Charles:** My extended family still isn't very accepting of Carole or Carole's children. My family has a summer camp that I helped my dad build. Being there together is one of our family traditions. While there, my mother wanted to take a photo of *her* grandchildren, excluding Trevor and Tyler. She just doesn't understand how hurtful that is to us as well as Trevor and Tyler. Tyler is 6'4". She refers to him only as "the tall one!" She never uses his name! Carole was included because, like it or not, she is my wife, but to this day inclusion of Carole and her boys has not fully happened.

JIM and NANCY

> **Nancy:** We lived less than half a mile from my folks. My boys were always welcome to use my parents' pool with their friends. One of my boys' favorite memories is being served grape juice and 'Nilla Wafers poolside. But whenever Jimmy asked if he could come over to swim with his friends, there was always a reason why the answer was "No."

> **Jim:** Whenever we joined Nancy's family for a special holiday, one of her sisters and some of her nieces were friendly with me and my daughters. Other nieces that were about the same age as Teri and

Karen were cool and aloof. Her brother-in-law was seemed unwilling to participate in friendly conversation with me. I felt like an unwanted, unimportant appendage to Nancy.

Nancy: After a few times when I noticed that my nieces were not warming up toward the girls, I told Teri and Karen, "You are always invited and always welcome to come to my family's events, but if you'd rather not be there, it's OK with me and your dad." It was several years before Teri and Karen were in my family circle again and were then treated with friendliness and inclusion.

Jim: I finally told Nancy that I didn't want to attend anymore when that brother-in-law would be present.

Nancy: I understood. This was *my* family...relationships that I wanted to maintain and a place where I was always welcome. We agreed that Jim would stay home unless it was an event where I particularly needed him to be with me.

Jim's family lives out of state. There were only rare instances when I would see them. One of the first was a few months after we married. His late wife Dixie's mother and two sisters came to visit for the afternoon. I was so aware of their graciousness to me in spite of their grief over Dixie's death. We all tried so hard it was exhausting. Jim, the girls, and Dixie's family were in the living room telling funny stories about Dixie... and laughing together. I knew it was healing for them and certainly not designed to make me uncomfortable. But I felt left out...not so much snubbed, but just sad at all the history I had missed with Jim and his children.

I, (Nancy) could have made an issue of my parents' exclusion of Jimmy and his friends. I didn't. Maybe I should have.

Charles could have requested a second photo be taken including Trevor and Tyler. I don't recall him saying that he did that.

Some of these extended family issues just won't go away by dictating that they disappear, or making a bigger issue out of them by fighting for things to be done "right." Others may require a discussion like the one below to decide if a boundary needs to be expressed to the offending party.

Some of these issues are cultural. Some cultures are far more inclusive of extra family members than others.

AN ESSENTIAL GUIDELINE

Each partner deals with his/her own family. The "new" wife or husband does not address these issues with their in-laws. This recommendation is wise for first-couples as well as step-couples. Emotionally getting in-between your partner and his/her parents (or the Ex!) is a formula for getting attacked by both and escalating the issue, rather than resolving it.

If your partner is unwilling to address an issue with his/her parents or extended family members, your best option is asking for a Skilled Discussion *with your partner, not* going behind his/her back to *take care of it* yourself!

WHEN CHILDREN ARE SNUBBED

One option is to explain to your child/ren that the slights are not his fault. She hasn't done anything wrong. That family is just having trouble adjusting to the changes in their family. It may get better over time, or it may not. "How can I help you manage your hurt? Or anger? Or feelings of rejection? What do you need from me?" Often just acknowledging the issue and reassuring that it isn't the child's fault is enough to soothe that child's feelings.

> **Nancy:** When my elder son died, and the family gathered at my parents' home after his memorial service, I noticed that my nieces were warm and welcoming to Teri and Karen. Time, and a shared grief had broken down the barriers of "this is my family...that family is yours." We all grieved together.

FRIENDS AND CONFIDANTES

Our words are powerful. Complaining about your current spouse or his/her children to someone who *takes your side* is short term gratification using a tactic that will eventually make the relationships worse. It's wise to avoid negative reports to your loving, prejudiced mom or dad or even a good friend. Some precious friends are evolved/conscious enough to listen to you venting your frustration, but won't take sides. Will, instead, perhaps ask for permission to give you advice about seeking good help, or even help you look at what you may be doing that *could* be changed.

Those friends are rare, however. Anyone who *takes your side* and fosters your blaming, accusing stance is someone who can't be trusted with the long-term welfare of you or your family.

The only exception is when you are in a relationship that is unsafe for you or your child. Then it is very appropriate to ask for help from a trusted friend or an organization that specializes in helping victims of abuse.

WHEN DEALING WITH AN EX (or others) CREATES PROBLEMS IN YOUR CURRENT RELATIONSHIP

Directions: Take turns completing the following sentences. When you've each had your turn sharing your preferred ground rules, use respectful speaking and listening skills to discuss any reactions you have to what you've heard. Continue the negotiations until you can agree on ground rules for dealing with your Ex/es.

She: I recommend that we adopt the following three ground rules for dealing with Exes:

_____
_____
_____

He: I recommend that we adopt the following three ground rules for dealing with Exes:

_____
_____
_____

Ground rules on which we agree:

_____
_____
_____

SUMMARY

The sanctity of the marriage (I know it's an old-fashioned term, but the *sanctity* of *this* marriage) needs to be reinforced with boundaries on other relationships that prevent outside persons from entering the sacred space of your marriage. If you still have emotional ties to that person, that union, get help from a wise counselor to complete the business of *that* marriage so that you can fully devote yourself to *this* marriage. Learn and practice skills and keep agreements that enable you to build trust and emotional security between you and your current partner.

BUILDING TASK

Schedule a date to talk about any boundaries that you'd like to see implemented in order to protect your current marriage and family. Be totally open to hearing the concerns of your partner whether or not you believe they are justified. Be willing to abide by boundaries that restore or strengthen your current marriage. If you find you are driven by guilt regarding the failure of your previous marriage, get help from a counselor or trusted advisor about how to forgive yourself, let go and move on.

COMING UP...

What happens when our treasured traditions collide with each other? How do we choose?

CHAPTER NINE: Colliding Traditions

Stepfamilies are not the only families that get caught in a holiday vise. Which family's gathering do you attend on Christmas Eve? Where do you go for Hannukkah celebration? Do you join his family on their yearly boating trip? Or her family's traditions for Labor Day Weekend? How do you juggle the desires of your extended families with your own family's needs?

My mother was especially poor at understanding how much pressure she put on her four daughters to give her what she wanted for any holiday. When my boys were little, she and Dad would show up at our house early Christmas morning and want us to open our gifts fast (she wanted the pleasure of seeing her two grandsons' excitement) so that they could leave for my sister's house. *They* were waiting to open *their* gifts until Grandma and Grandpa arrived.

I finally suggested that they might alternate which home they went to on any particular year. I (and my boys) didn't want to be rushed. We wanted Christmas morning to be leisurely...enjoyable. And we would join my folks later for the big family gathering. Sigh...

The pressure becomes exponentially increased with the extended relatives in a stepfamily.

Traditions are a large part of the framework that reassures us that all is well and gives our lives stability. Traditions may include foods, family visits, entertaining, friends, trips, religious practice, clothing, photographs, activities, recreation. Traditions also include mundane routines such as greetings and goodbye habits, always doing the laundry on Mondays or washing the car on Saturday mornings.

Sometimes we think of these things as small until we discover that our spouse or his/her children have very different traditions that clash or interfere with ours. There may be traditions/routines that are easy for you to let go of but which mean a great deal to your child. The loss of a tradition may add to the losses your child is mourning.

I'm including in this chapter the *Holiday Survival Guide for Stepfamilies*. The strategies outlined in this article can be used to navigate any potentially hurtful change in traditions for the whole family. I've been told by those who've followed the instructions that it's very practical for working out how to give each of your children (and you!) the most precious of your winter holiday experiences. The process will give you some valuable ideas for addressing other traditions that may be important for you or your child to continue to enjoy the traditions that are the most important to you.

Note: All of these strategies work for a nuclear family, (meaning a first marriage with no children from a previous relationship) but they are particularly great for stepfamilies because the dynamics of stepfamilies around the holidays is exponentially more pressure packed!

Part #1: TRADITION!

Remember the opening solo Tevya sings in the musical, *Fiddler on the Roof*? **TRADITION!** Traditions are a framework providing structure for the family. **Traditions reassure us, but especially children, that all is well, that life is secure.**

Stepfamilies suffer more than the average number of upsets in traditions. Where will which child be on Christmas Eve? Which parent or grandparent expects which child for Christmas day? How will we celebrate the days of Hanukkah? And in which home? **When will *we* get to celebrate as a family?** When do we open gifts? What food will be served? PJ's and popcorn balls on Christmas Eve or a Candlelight Service at midnight? Which sweets can be eliminated? And which ones are essential to complete our sense of holiday? Who's going to do the cooking? And when will there be *time*? Etc., etc., etc.!

You take *your* traditions for granted...they are "normal," until your new spouse expects to celebrate the holidays his/her way. Schedules are complicated by an Ex's demand for time with your child, or a Grandparent "must have *their*" grandchildren over to make cookies.

This guide will help you through this maze of conflicting demands in a way that will enable you to Survive the Holidays with a minimum of stress...and perhaps even some genuine joy!

Start with **THE HOLIDAY TRADITION TREASURE HUNT**. This step builds the foundation for every other step in this Guide. These are the instructions: You and your partner each **list your respective "normal" ways of celebrating**. List everything. Relatives visited. Favorite foods served. A tree or no tree. Presents: quality or quantity. Religious services attended. Where. Any special games or routines with the children. Gifts opened when? Be especially careful to list the traditions you Treasure.

DO NOT DISCUSS THESE LISTS UNTIL THE NEXT STEP! No judging about what tradition is a "have-to!" or comments about "We can't do that *then* because...." Just make your lists.

Don't get up tight about this. **THE TREASURE HUNT** *can* be fun and *could* be completed in one evening. **THE TRADITION TREASURE HUNT WORKSHEET** below will help you.

Then each of you, (partners) on your own list of traditions, assign a number (1-3) next to each tradition. **#1 is a must keep for you. #2 is negotiable. #3 is OK if it gets lost.**

Now each parent takes your list to each of your birth children. Say something like, "There have been a lot of changes in our family. **I want to find out which holiday things in the past have really meant the most to you** so I can try to make sure they're included again this year." Ask them to assign numbers to the traditions that are 1s, 2s or 3s for them. They can add a tradition if you left it out.

Your child may want something that is impossible to give, such as "I love climbing into bed with you and Dad on Christmas morning." Or, "I want us to go back to being our old family." When the "ask" is out of the question, **respond with understanding for how bad it feels to have lost that tradition**. Offer comfort.

You and your partner now **put all of the #1s of the whole family on a separate list** with the person's name or initials beside the tradition.

Lighting the Menorah with Grandma and Grandpa. Sam, Jonas and Mary want to attend he Christmas Eve Candlelight Service.

Susan and Tommy want Christmas Eve at home, popping popcorn, wearing pajamas and watching a movie.

Danny wants to open the presents on Christmas morning.

Mary has a particular food that makes Hanukka her favorite holiday and making a gingerbread house with Grandma.

Or...

Add all of the #2s and who wants each #2.

Skip the #3s! Yay!

The goal is to find a way so that everyone in the family gets as many as possible of their #1 traditions...**things that "make" the holiday for them.** Plus a few #2s if possible.

Complete **The HOLIDAY TRADITIONS TREASURE HUNT Worksheet** in the next 24 hours so you'll be ready for Part #3.

But first, it's essential to do Part #2 *before* you can successfully move on to Part #3. *As you collect each person's #1 and #2, do not judge or make decisions about what can or can't be included.*

The HOLIDAY TRADITIONS TREASURE HUNT Worksheet

1. **Make three copies of this page.**
2. Each partner fills out **one copy listing ALL of the holiday traditions that mean the most to you.** AFTER the list is completed, go back and assign each a number:
   - **#1 for a "Cannot live without,"**
   - **#2 for "Maybe negotiable,"**
   - **#3 for "OK if this gets dropped."**

TRADITIONS: RATINGS BY EACH PERSON WITH THEIR INITIAL:

3. Go to each of your birth children with your list. **If you forgot something that is important to a child, add it**. Ask the child to rank each of the traditions, #1-3. Do not pressure the child to assign ranks like yours. You may not have any idea which tradition that is forgettable for you is a precious treasure in your child's memory bank!

DON'T QUIT NOW! IT'S ABOUT TO GET EXCITING!

4. Use the third copy of **THE HOLIDAY TRADITIONS TREASURE HUNT** to compile the family's #1s and #2s. **List all of the #1s first**, with the family members initials to the side who voted that tradition a #1.
List all of the #2s next with the family members initials to the side who voted that tradition a #2. Forget the #3s.
5. **CELEBRATE!** Whew! Pat yourselves on the back! Exchange high-fives all around! Grab a cup of cocoa and watch a movie. **You've just laid the foundation for how to Survive the Holidays as a Stepfamily!**
6. Part #3 of the **Holiday Survival Guide for Stepfamilies** will show you HOW to fit in a minimum of one #1 desire for each family member (and probably much more!) without adding to your holiday stress!
7. But first do not skip Part #2! Do it *before* going on to Part #3!

Part #2: HOLIDAY RULES TO BREAK!

Our culture is full of expectations that get turned into rules set in concrete. Christmas happens only on December 25th. Every family has a Christmas tree. Grandparents and Aunt Mabel must be included in our holiday meal. The neighbors must get homemade cookies. Everyone must attend the religious service of your choice. Etc., Etc., Etc.!

No wonder that a few years ago **when November 1st showed up on my calendar my heart sank!** I didn't know how I could survive the holidays! The year before I'd sewn 17 different clothing and quilted items to give to my family members in order to save money. I'd baked over 400 Gingies (our family's favorite cookie) to dispense to everyone we knew.

As I felt myself sliding into dread and apprehension, I asked myself, "Do I really want to drive myself to exhaustion and resentment again? How can I do this differently?" A loud answer came from inside, **"I WON'T DO THAT AGAIN!"** My first decision was that I would not do anything I resented doing. I would only do what gave me joy. I began looking for ways to "break the holiday rules" I'd unconsciously accepted as sacrosanct!

Rule #1 to Break: You can declare any day, or combination of days, to be "Christmas" or "Hanukkah!" **What if you decide that The Holidays last from December 10th through December 30th?** You may be limited to a few activities that are only available on certain dates, but others can be spread out over those 20 days!

Meet Aunt Mabel for coffee and a brownie before the school play. If the Ex insists on having the children on Christmas Day, then declare December 27th as YOUR Christmas Day! If the Ex or extended family want the children to sleep over for a few days, then **you and your partner have a staycation** during the days your children are gone, and have your celebration with them the following week. (WhooHoo! Home Alone!)

You get the idea. Loosen up the brain cells. Think outside the box. **Break the rules or at least make the rules fit** what is do-able with the least amount of stress!

Rule #2 to Break: Everyone must be happy or the holiday is a bust! How unrealistic is that? How impossible to make that happen! Are you a magician? There's no magic wand that will create this outcome...in any family, let alone a stepfamily. **Decide that your people-pleasing compulsions get put in the bottom drawer on December 1st and are unavailable to you until sometime next year!** You're doing every reasonable thing you can do for those closest to you by discovering your family's #1 Holiday Treasures. But you can't take the next step without breaking Rules #1 and #2.

Rule #3 to Break: Everyone must be at every event or we're not a "real" family. Stepfamilies can't always show up in lock-step with each other. One of the most impossible unrealistic expectations for you is that you should function like a nuclear family! **Just because you don't always look like the fictional "all-American" family, doesn't mean you're failing as a family,** but demonstrating flexibility over unrealistic conformity. Sometimes you must go one place with your children and your partner must go to another event with his or her children.

DOES BREAKING THE RULES BRING ON HEART PALPITATIONS? BREATHE! YOU CAN DO THIS!

The following worksheet will help you shush the inner critic's objections about breaking the rules.

YES! <u>DO</u> Break These Rules!

On A scale of 1-10, what was your stress level during the last holiday season? _____

What were the primary sources of your stress? Rate each of these possibilities.

	Lack of Time		Family Obligations
	Wanting to Please Everyone		Trying to Fit Everything In
	Decorating		Cooking/Baking Expectations
	Shopping/Money		Exhaustion

	Relationship Conflicts		Other
	Doing Things I Dislike		ALL of the Above!

What were the rules that contributed to your stress?

	I want the Traditional look and feel of the holidays.		I have to please my relatives. Show up at traditional events and be happy.
	I want my family to look like a Norman Rockwell painting…happy, loving, together.		I must do it all myself…great food, perfect presents, cookies for all.
	The house and yard must look festive.		Events should be celebrated by the calendar.
	Everyone I care about must get a gift. (Co-workers, extended family, neighbors.)		The children must get what they most want. No matter the cost.
	I want to look and feel like/be a "normal" family.		Religious services must be included.
	I'll worry about the money later.		Other:
	Other:		Other:

Would cutting your stress in half be worth challenging a few of these rules?

Draw a line through the rules that seem the most impossible for you to challenge or change.

Which person/s in your family or friends will **present the biggest challenge to you** if you don't meet their expectations?

Are you afraid of their displeasure? Or disappointing them? What's the worst that could happen?

How hard have you been trying to make your stepfamily look or act like a nuclear, "normal" family? **Would it be a relief to you to know that your goal is impossible?** Stepfamilies have very complex dynamics that usually make it impossible to duplicate a "regular" family. (In fact, have you noticed that many nuclear families don't seem very "normal"?)

In the next step, you'll have a chance to **plan strategies that may greatly decrease your stress level**, or even make it possible to thrive during this holiday season!

Part #3: The Treasure Map

So, you're ready to break a few crazy, unrealistic rules. Good for you! **It's time to create a map** to lead you through to the treasure of a holiday season that runs smoothly and doesn't leave you feeling resentful and worn out.

Step One: Make a date with your partner. Spread out a big calendar for the month of December. It's easier to see the whole month at once, rather than flipping through the pages on your cell phone or laptop calendars. (I recommend you take a paper calendar of December for the current year to a print shop to **have it enlarged** to make it easier to fit in all the names and events.)

Step Two: <u>With a pencil</u>**, put the "can't change" dates on the calendar:** Your kid's school programs, a church event, an unavoidable family commitment. Then add which persons must attend that event. (**Not which persons you want, wish, hope could attend, but which persons are the essential ones.** In the case of your child's school program, that child and the parent of that child are essential. Others are not, unless the child specifically expresses a strong desire for a sibling or the step-parent.) A pencil rather than a pen makes it easier to rearrange events until everything fits.

Step Three: Transfer your family's #1 items onto the calendar. Begin brainstorming how each can be accommodated. Remember, **you are not tied down to any particular date!** Make sure that each person in the family has at least one of their #1 wants on the calendar! Set aside a couple of hours at least twice during this month for a fun couple date! (This is not for shopping. It's for FUN!)

Step Four: Add the expectations or requests of your Exes on the calendar and which children are affected. Add any obligations that are important to grandparents or extended family members. (Remember **you are in charge of when and where and how you meet the requests of your extended family or friends.** This may mean turning down a non-essential dinner date or event with friends. It may mean explaining to grandparents that the demands of your new stepfamily have complicated the holidays. "It's important for us to see you. The time it would work best for us is _____. Can we come by then for (whatever length of time you can give)?" Don't take it personally if they're unhappy about being further down the priority line than they may wish to be! Remain kind, but firm.

Step Five: See how many of your #2 items can be fitted to the calendar, either individually or combined with another event while making sure **at least two (or three, or four) nights/week are left free of any obligation**. Remember, not every family member needs to be present for every event.

Step Six: Work your plan! Remain flexible, (a child gets sick, one of you has to work late one night) but don't change your plans when someone is pouting because you turned down an invitation to their open house, or have to see them combined with Aunt Mabel rather than a special evening with them alone. **Remember, be respectful but people-pleasing is on hold!**

Step Seven: Survive the holidays, yes. But more than that, ENJOY THEM! Congratulate yourselves! You did the work! You worked your plan! You've even enjoyed yourselves!

Step #4: Slay the Holiday Money Monster!

One of the biggest areas that create conflict between step-partners is money. The **Money Monster raises its head with a vengeance around holiday spending.**

Ted and Julie were in my stepfamily class. A few weeks before they were on the **verge of separating** because the fighting was so pernicious and unrelenting! Mainly about different parenting styles and money.

They had agreed on a budget for kids' gifts and expenses, but then **each, behind the back of the other, was spending** extra money on his or her children. (This is typical step-couple behavior!)

They realized they were putting their marriage at risk by going behind each other's backs, invalidating their previous agreement. They worked out a budget that allowed equal amounts for each child's gifts for birthdays and Christmas. Money spent on extracurricular activities was negotiated with each other. They understood, as they never had before, that keeping their agreements with each other was essential to rebuilding trust between them and securing their love for each other into the future.

A huge part of **The Holiday Survival Guide for Stepfamilies** is working out a total budget for the family expenditures, with a specific amount to be spent on gifts for each child and each other. **Imagine a January without a blow up about maxed out credit cards, or purchases that violated your agreements.** No exceptions. No excuses. If an unforeseen circumstance comes up requiring money, you negotiate it with each other BEFORE any changes are made in the plan.

A little bit of work now, an agreement that you are both committed to keeping, and then actually reining in your impulsive buying and staying within the limits you agreed to, will give you, if not a totally lush January, **at least a January without the bitter after-taste of betrayal.**

This plan works even if your incomes are unequal, or your resources extremely different...such as pinched vs. rolling in dough. You take that into consideration as you map out your plan.

Use the following **Slay the Holiday Money Monster** worksheet to help you get through the holidays feeling great about yourselves!

SLAY THE HOLIDAY MONEY MONSTER WORKSHEET

The goal of this exercise is to prevent money-based blow-ups during or after the holidays. It's to encourage cooperation and accountability. **The biggest goal is to build your belief in yourselves as a great team!**

This is the time to **share your beliefs or expectations about holiday giving.** Does one of you think money is no object? Pleasing the child is most important? Does one of you believe in stringent budgets?

If you have separate bank accounts, are you willing to **agree on a standard amount for each of your children to avoid inequities in gifts?** Do you each have an amount you're each willing to contribute to holiday expenses? If so, you can use a simple notebook to keep track of your deposits and withdrawals.

If your money is pooled, do you have a holiday savings account? If so, how much is in that account? If there are no holiday savings can **you agree on a total amount to be divvied up between all holiday expenses?** How much will come from cash? How much will you agree can be added to a credit card?

Decide on how much to spend on each other times two. How much to spend on each child, multiplied by the number of children. Will an allowance be given to each child so they can purchase something for their other birth parent? If so, how much? **Will you be doing entertaining?** Or helping to supply meal ingredients? Or providing one or more dishes to a group celebration?

Are you traveling for the holidays? Airfare? Hotels? Gas?

Is baking cookies for extended family or neighbors or co-workers a practice you just can't give up? (I **buy supplies in bulk at a discount grocery store** to bake my family's favorite Gingies. MUCH less expensive that way!)

Some awesome gifts can be found **in charity or consignment shops**. Make sure items are clean and sticker free! Pretty wrapping paper and ribbon dress up any gift.

Is there a holiday movie or concert that you'd like to share with your family? Will the children be welcome to bring guests? Can snacks be packed from home?

Making these decisions ahead of time prevents you from giving in to last minute begging, and enables you to keep your agreements with each other that **Slay the Money Monster!**

Expenditure:	$ Amount:	Multiplied Times:	Subtotal:
Partner Gifts			
Children Gifts			
Children's Gift Allowances			
Extended Family Gifts			
Entertainment Budget			
Special Events			
Other			
After Holiday Discount Shopping			
			TOTAL:

If your subtotals add up to a bigger TOTAL than you can swing or are comfortable with, **you may need to work backward from the total amount you're willing to spend.** Then divide it up between the categories. If that's what you decide to do, then brainstorm how the holiday can feel festive within your limited funds. Get creative! Think outside the box! Give handmade, but colorful gift certificates for generous gifts of actions. (A car wash? Doing the laundry for a week? A four-hour gift of free time to do anything the receiver wants?)

Some amazing bargains can be found, particularly on holiday decorations and gift wrap, in the last week of the year. **Do you want to include some money for post-holiday shopping?** One friend on a tight budget gave her daughter a nice gift to open on Christmas Day AND a gift certificate to Macy's to spend at the after-holiday sales! Her money went much further that way.

Remember your goal…to cooperate on holiday spending so there is no negative fall-out in January that damages your marriage!

THEN…

Part #5: Review & Future Planning

December 31st is the time to evaluate. How did the **Holiday Survival Guide** work for you? I want to hear. Let me know by going to Facebook: Nancy Landrum Author Relationship Coach. Or message me on my website: www.nancylandrum.com

What parts of your plan reduced your stress the most? _____

_____

What parts of it fell apart in the chaos of holiday demands? _____

_____

_____

What can you do better next year? _____

_____

If a fight erupted, what was it about? _____

_____

What part of the plan, if implemented, might have helped to avoid the fight? _____

_____

Put this **Holiday Survival Guide for Stepfamilies** in a place where you'll find it next year by November 1st. Save the **Holiday Treasure Map**. Next year you'll have a jump-start on planning for successful, low-stress holidays!

★   ★   ★

Although I targeted the December holidays, **these strategies work for any event** or vacation or holiday that puts pressure on the already pressure packed dynamics of a stepfamily.

How can this guide be used to plan other special occasions?_____

_____

Weekend or Three-day Weekend Routines:
Picnics? Eating out? Special Breakfasts?
Dress up? Or Casual?
Recreational Activities?
Camping? Travel?
Backyard Barbeques? Entertaining?
House cleaning/laundry routines?
Religious Service Attendance?
Yard chores?
Volunteer Service Work?
Sports: for yourself? Children?
Special bedtimes? T.V. Shows?
Other:_____

Birthday Traditions:
A Cake? What kind? Store bought? Homemade?
One big gift? Many smaller gifts?
A party? With Family? Friends? Peers?
At home? In a restaurant? A park?
Decorations? Surprises?
Traditions around certain ages? 12? 15? 16? 21?
Ceremonies?
Other:_____

Stumbling Blocks to Successfully Establishing New Traditions:
_____   Taking it personally when a child wants to be with his/her bio-parent rather than stepparent on special holidays.
_____   Having hurt feelings when the child only remembers the bio-parent on holidays.
_____   Measuring traditions as better or worse than others.
_____   Making a child feel guilty about wanting the traditions that are important to him/her.
_____   Judging the "other" parent's ways of doing things as "bad" or "wrong."

Building Blocks to Successfully Establishing New Traditions:
_____   Well ahead of a holiday, having a family meeting to find out or ask each member what traditions are important.
_____   Working out a plan where each person's favorite tradition is honored.
_____   Acknowledging the difficulty of making changes in traditions.
_____   Showing Understanding for the sadness that sometimes comes with change.
_____   Asking each child what is important to do for his/her birthday.
_____   Planning a way for the child to honor the non-resident parent on days such as Father's Day/Mother's Day, the other parent's birthday, etc.

SUMMARY

As one of the step-moms said, the devil is in the details. Sometimes we are unaware that a tradition that is important to a child has been overlooked until it doesn't happen as the child expects and there are hurt feelings or anger. Traditions that may seem insignificant to you, may have enormous significance to your child...particularly when so many other things have changed. Do your best to ask, anticipate and provide the traditions that provide a sense of security and continuity for yourself and your child.

My son Peter (age 13) complained that everything was changing. He didn't like it. I understood. It was like we were on a runaway train. Things happened so quickly. I couldn't anticipate what would be OK and what would hurt him.

Then he asked if he could go camping with his friend's family over the Thanksgiving holiday. I knew and trusted the family, so I said, "Sure!" Then I added, "This is a tradition that *you* want to change. I've never been away from you over Thanksgiving. I'll miss you. But I understand and want you to have a great time."

Change is just part of life. But there are multiple changes that happen when a stepfamily is formed with little time to adjust. Try to have compassion for yourself and your family members who need time to assimilate the changes...or may need to complain or rebel against too many, too soon!

Many of our family traditions have changed, evolved, been transformed over time. It's just the nature of a growing family with changing needs. After Jim passed, I noticed that our family didn't get together as often. Jim seemed to be the hub around which our family operated. The love and respect between me and my step-children is still there in abundance, but I don't see them as often as before Jim's death. My son and his step-siblings still communicate with each other, and even attend the most important events of the others' families, but we no longer get together to celebrate Christmas or birthdays.

An adjustment for me is to accept that this doesn't mean failure on my part...or a lack of love from any of us. It only means our circumstances and needs have changed.

BUILDING TASK:

Ask, ask, ask. Don't assume that you know what is important to your family members. Traditions are like comfort food, reassuring us that some part of our foundation is still intact. What special event is coming up that you can use the questions above to help clarify expectations? Be prepared to offer comfort if a child's favorite tradition is now impossible to continue. (Like cuddling in bed with both his birth parents.)

Coming up...

How do you parent in a way that builds a strong and secure child? Some tips...

STEPPING TWOGETHER: BUILDING A SECURE CHILD

Every parent wishes for the magic formula that enables the building of a resilient and secure child. This section provides some hints about how to do that in a stepfamily.

CHAPTER TEN: Meeting the Needs of My Child

There's no way I could possibly do justice to the topic of healthy child rearing in this book. This and the next few chapters are attempts to touch on a few of the most basic tools or guidelines generally agreed as important and point out practices that are especially important in a stepfamily.

I once heard this definition of a "good parent:" One who is willing to sacrifice in order to meet the needs of his/her child. Correspondingly, a "bad parent" is one who uses the child to meet his or her needs.

Each of us lives somewhere on the continuum between a "good parent" and a "bad parent." In fact, in one day, we may exhibit traits of both!

Parenting in a step-family often requires sacrifice from both the bio-parent and the step-parent in order to meet the most essential needs of a child. Then the question of every caring parent is, "What *are* the most essential needs? And *how* do I make sure I'm meeting those needs?"

Those questions, especially in times of crisis or transition, reveal the most haunting insecurities of many parents.

Am I making the right decision about ___? Has the death of her other parent, (or the divorce of her parents) irrevocably scarred her for life? Am I giving a healthy balance of permissiveness and discipline to him? What does loving a child mean, anyway? How do I do it? Will my child eventually resent me? Hate me? Blame me?

Perhaps some of the following tidbits of information touching on parenting, and especially parenting in a stepfamily, will give you some specific guidelines to help answer those questions.

Becoming a better parent requires becoming a better me. In many cases that means learning better communication skills, then using those respectful skills with my child as well as my partner. Becoming more self-disciplined. Doing everything I can to make this marriage work well. Doing what cast-member Charles calls, "the hard, right thing" rather than the "easy, wrong thing." It means working hard at developing the best possible relationship with the child's other bio-parent. Or, honoring the memory of a deceased parent. Modeling character traits that you hope your child will adopt. Setting boundaries and enforcing consequences when it isn't fun...or popular.

As much effort as we put into doing a good job parenting, there is no such thing as a perfect parent...and ultimately, each child may make some choices that we never anticipated and of which we don't approve. We must share responsibility for the outcome with the child who, eventually, makes his or her own decisions and, hopefully, those choices will lead them to a productive, happy life.

The following are primarily about parenting minor-aged children. There will be more about possible challenges with adult children in CHAPTER THIRTEEN.

Exercise: Imagine yourself to be inside the world of your most difficult bio-child (if you have more than one). Speak as your child, telling your partner what it is like living in this family.

Example: I as (child's name) think that..._____

I feel ... and ... and ..._____

I am worried about..._____

I am afraid that..._____

I wish that..._____

I like it when..._____

Partner: Repeat back what you've heard in your own words. As you listen, try to get into the world of this child and experience it through his/her eyes.

If you both have a biological child, trade places.

Although you may not know for certain the thoughts, feelings or worries of your child without asking him or her, what did you learn from putting yourself in the place of your child?

THE TWO BOOKENDS OF SECURITY:

#1, Nurturing a loving bond plus #2, being consistent about rules and consequences are the two bookends that help a child feel secure. Note: The more secure the loving bond, the less need for corrective actions.

Loving, emotional connection is created and increased by:

Affectionate touch.

Simply enjoying your child and letting them know you enjoy them.

Encouraging words.

Listening with empathy, caring about their experience.

Spending time with them, doing *with* them what they enjoy.

Dependable routines (greeting rituals, nighttime routines, etc.)

Being there during important times for them.

Acknowledging and appreciating their efforts and accomplishments.

Supporting the child's relationship with the other bio-parent.

Making your goals for them clear. (For instance: be a self-disciplined, responsible, caring adult.)

Since becoming a stepfamily, what "together" things have I ceased doing with my child? What does she wish I would do with her? _____

Have I given my child a chance to say what he is feeling? How do I respond when he tells me how he feels?_____
_____

What is one thing I can do this week that would mean a lot to her?
_____

What words does he need to hear from me? _____

The acronym **DISCIPLINE** contains a few more elements that nurture a secure child…

Disclose both your struggles and triumphs with self-discipline.

Instruct and expect age appropriate behaviors. Self-discipline is the goal. Start with the end in mind.

Consequences must be consistent. Keep your word.

Inspire by asking questions, telling stories, using examples.

Participate in your child's interests and validate feelings.

Look for opportunities to express love in your child's love language.

Inform yourself about today's pre-teen and teen culture.

Notice opportunities to encourage, praise and reward.

Evaluate yourself and your child every few months.

D is for Disclose: Be real! Share some of the ways you have not been self-disciplined and how that has hurt you. Share some of the ways you are still learning self-discipline and what you see as the benefit. If you're not disciplined or working on becoming more self-disciplined, how can you expect it of your child?

Example: "We are working to learn better ways of communicating. I'm practicing until these skills become more habitual. It's work. But it's paying off because we are fighting less, we are treating each other more respectfully. We are working to resolve the issues that trouble us and affect you. We have to follow rules and be responsible for the way we treat each other and you. I won't ask you to do anything that I am not doing myself." Post on the bathroom

mirror or share, "This week I (we) learned…." Don't: Disclose private things about yourself or others. Don't run down others. Don't compare your child to someone else's negatively.

I is for Instruct: What are some age appropriate behaviors and skills for various ages?

Example: Instruct a four-year old about how to put toys away after play. Make it a game. Do it with them. A twelve-year old is capable of putting things away, but may need help learning how to do laundry or venting emotions in a way that doesn't hurt self or others. A sixteen-year old is capable of understanding the need to come home when agreed, or call, but may need help learning to parallel park. A twenty-year old is able to make most decisions alone, yet may ask for your opinion about whether to complete school or join the army. Don't punish a child for doing something poorly if you haven't taught them how to do it. Don't punish for mistakes that anyone could make.

S is for Self-Discipline: The more gains a child makes in self-discipline, the less need to handle disciplinary problems. To be self-disciplined is to follow of your own accord—to see personal value in the course that is chosen—not about being forced by someone else or the threat of punishment. A self-disciplined twenty-year old will treat others with respect, make choices that support his/her goals and be a contributing member of the family and society.

Example: When a child has learned caring behavior toward others, the value of turning assignments in on time, the satisfaction of occasionally having a clean room, the reward of being thoughtful, the benefit of making and saving money…that child will continue to make choices that benefit himself and others around him.

Don't: Require a disciplined lifestyle to the degree of being rigidly regimented. That extreme of perfectionism often blows up in out-of-control rebellion later, or results in a judgmental intolerance of others which pushes others away.

C is for Consequences: Make the consequences fit the mis-step.

Example: If the rule is to do homework before television or phone calls and you find the TV on or Junior on the phone, unplug the TV and put it in the garage for a few days. Lock the cell phone away for a day or two. Be matter-of-fact. "Sorry, son, this is the consequence of the choice you made." (Refer to House Rules in CHAPTER SIX) If your ten-year old daughter throws a tantrum, take her aside or to her room and begin skilled listening until she calms down. Then tell her next time she feels ready to burst, to ask for listening, rather than inflicting her raging emotions on everyone around her. Or give her a pillow to punch!

Don't: be a pushover or an ogre. Don't make threats you know you can't or won't back up. State a consequence once, and then follow through with the action. Do not be extreme in your consequences. Your goal is not to torture, but to teach. Don't be overly emotional when following through. If you are very emotional, give yourself a "time out" before dealing with the issue. The 'respect 24/7 rule' (taught in the Millionaire Marriage Club) applies with your child, too!

I is for Inspire: Be open about the purpose of your efforts. You want your child to have the qualities and habits that will make his adult life as functional and productive as possible. Use everyday examples to teach. Make a game of guessing what qualities may have been necessary to take a man to a starring position on a football team or made it possible for a woman to earn a Masters Degree. Look for ways to help your child succeed in things that mean a lot to him or her.

Example: Johnny comes home bummed because his friend got expelled for bringing drugs on campus. Ask, "Why do you think he did that? What other choices has he made that led him here? What other choices did he have?" If your divorce has caused your daughter a lot of pain, tell her, "I made some poor choices. I didn't know how to solve problems in a respectful way. Until I took this class, I didn't understand how much my behavior contributed to the problems we had. I'm learning now. I don't ever want to put you through something like that again so I'm working hard to change my bad relationship habits."

Don't: Use the inspiration of others' accomplishments to put your child down or expect similar accomplishments that don't fit your child's interests or aptitudes.

P is for Participate: There is convincing evidence that the stronger the parent-child bond, the more empathic the child is. The more empathic a child (or adult), the less there will be disciplinary problems. An empathic person is not likely to do things to others that cause pain. With children, bonding occurs when you play (participate) on their level—enjoy doing with them what they enjoy doing. Bonding occurs when they can express feelings and be heard and understood.

Example: One mother hated the excessive time her son spent playing video games. It was suggested that she ask him to teach her how to play and to play with him for fifteen minutes a day. It wasn't long before asking him to quit playing so he could get to his homework was met with "OK" rather than a fight. Of course, playing with him was paired with the understanding that the video game would be locked up for 3 days if he didn't move on to his homework. But it was the playing with him that strengthened the emotional bond between them.

Don't: Judge feelings as bad or suggest they are wrong to feel a particular way. Don't judge the interests of a kid to be silly, just because they don't agree with your interests. Find ways to support your kid's aptitudes.

L is for Look: Observe your child. Study him or her. What are her likes? What maintains his interest?

Example: Like adults, children have different love languages. You may be giving gifts when your child would prefer some uninterrupted time with you. Ask your child what behaviors of yours cause him or her to feel the most loved.

Don't: Be affectionate in situations where it is likely to embarrass or humiliate.

Inform yourself about today's pre-teen and teen culture. Unfortunately, the ways that children can be dangerously influenced have multiplied with the computer and other communication devices

Example: Be truthful that part of your responsibility as a parent is to know the friends, music, Facebook posts and website visits of your child. One mother of an impetuous 14-year-old girl I know finally gave in to her daughter's desire for a Facebook account. The condition for this privilege is that the mother is the only one who knows the password. Therefore, the mother must sign in each time the girl wants to visit and has access to the account to see her daughter's choice of friends and the contents of the messages. Of course, the girl thinks it's unfair and "You don't trust me." The mom just says, "Those are my conditions. Take it or leave it."

Don't: go to the extreme of being paranoid, suspicious and constantly eavesdropping as though you are just waiting to "catch" your kid in misbehavior. Make it clear that trust will be given as trust is earned. Trust is earned by small steps done well. And some opportunities have the potential for far too much danger to entrust to anyone under 18!

Notice opportunities to encourage, praise and reward. If misbehaviors are the only ones that are rewarded with attention, then misbehaviors will multiply.

Example: Here is another opportunity to fit your praise to the child. Some children prefer a quiet, "Great job." Others want a lot of hoop-lah! Some are motivated by money. Some are motivated by knowing they've pleased you. Give encouragement and praise in the form that means the most to your child. But do notice and reward!

Don't: praise only in front of guests or extended family (that feels to the child that it's more about attention for you) but do brag whenever you can.

Evaluate yourself and your child. What patterns of interaction are happening? Is the job getting done? What might be limiting your effectiveness? How self-disciplined are you in the parenting of your child? We can only give what we have. Don't carry out disciplinary actions when you are angry. Wait until you and the situation calm down.

BELIEFS THAT BLOCK EFFECTIVE PARENTING:

Unrealistic expectations in regard to stepfamily relationships.

Guilt for the failure of a marriage or for poor parenting choices in the past.

Fear of being rejected or of making the same mistakes your parents did or fear of the consequences of dealing with a tough issue.

Resentment toward the child's other parent (going over-board to make up for the other parent's failings) or toward your stepchildren or because your children have it so much easier than you did.

Unresolved grief for the death of a loved one or the loss of a marriage through divorce or for the child's loss of a parent due to death or your poor choice of a partner (their other parent). If necessary, get support to help you weed out feelings that result in pity and poor choices. Guilt and excessive regrets block your ability to make clear and effective parenting choices.

Pity. Beware of pity. Pity is weakening and crippling in its outcome. Get counseling or clergy help resolving grief or guilt about past choices or circumstances.

Fair, consistent discipline is empowering in its outcome.

One way to see if you're making bad decisions based on these emotions is to ask yourself these questions: "When he's twenty will his boss or a policeman excuse this behavior?" or "Is the behavior I'm allowing ultimately help him to have a good life?"

Self-Assessment of my Parenting Effectiveness

Disclose your own struggles to be more self-disciplined. Be real.

What are some things I can share about my life in the past or present to use as teaching opportunities?

Instruct and expect age appropriate behavior and skills.

For my child's age, what is reasonable to expect? Do I need to research stages child development?

Self-discipline is the goal. Start with the end in mind.

What do I want to be true about my child by adulthood?

Am I actively building those qualities into my child in ways appropriate for his/her age?

Consequences must be consistent. Keep your word.

Do I back up? Change my mind? Frequently?   If so, what is my child really learning?

Inspire by asking questions, telling stories, using examples.

What opportunities are in front of me that I can use as teaching moments?

Participate in your child's interests and validate feelings. ?   How might I participate with my child?

Am I paying more attention to my partner or stepchildren than to my own child? ?   How do I respond to his/her feelings?

Look for opportunities to express love.

Do I know what makes my child feel the most loved? (See **Love Languages for Kids** and **Love Languages for Teens** by Gary Chapman.) If so, can I discipline myself to deliver my love in that way rather than the way that is more comfortable for me?

Inform yourself about today's pre-teen and teen culture.

If appropriate, have I made it my business to know the words of songs, the websites and other things that influence my child?

What can I do today to become better informed?

Notice opportunities to encourage, praise and reward.

Discover what form of encouragement works best for your child. Use it!

Evaluate yourself and your child every few months.

Stumbling Blocks to a Successful Bio-Parent/Child Bond:

_____ Assuming my relationship to my bio-child is secure and more attention must be paid to the new relationships with a stepchild or spouse.
_____ Being pressured into decisions that don't feel right to me about my bio-child.
_____ Excusing my child from house rules others have to follow.
_____ Assuming my child will adjust.
_____ Excluding my spouse from relationship building activities with my child.
_____ Criticizing my spouse's efforts to connect with my child.
_____ Pushing my child into a relationship with the stepparent.
_____ Expecting the stepparent to take over unpleasant "discipline."

Building Blocks to a Successful Bio-Parent/Child bond:

_____ Remembering my primary responsibility is to my own child.
_____ Knowing that I am the ultimate authority over my own child.
_____ Spending time maintaining my unique relationship with my child.
_____ Encouraging the relationship of my child with the other bio-parent.
_____ Insisting that respectful behavior be given to stepparent and step-siblings.
_____ Enforcing agreed upon house rules and consequences if broken.
_____ Being the discipline deliverer for my child.
_____ Verbally transferring authority to my spouse when I'm not present.
_____ Listening by Showing Understanding for my child's feelings.
_____ Believing my child when he/she expresses fear or distrust.
_____ Paying attention to drastic changes in behavior.
_____ Trusting my gut.
_____ Reassuring of my love.
_____ Reassuring my child that the breakup or loss was not caused by him/her.

Stumbling Blocks to Effective Discipline in a Stepfamily:

_____ Forcing each other into opposite positions on the authoritarian/permissive scale.
_____ Thinking that my perspective is the only "right" one for this child or step-child.
_____ Forming an alliance with my child against my spouse or former spouse.
_____ Allowing a child to "play" one parent or stepparent against the other.
_____ Over-reacting, yelling, moralizing, preaching, embarrassing, criticizing or ignoring.
_____ Making exceptions to the rules without checking with my spouse.

Building Blocks to Effective Discipline in a Stepfamily:

_____ Recognizing that neither very authoritarian nor very permissive styles work well.
_____ Transferring authority from myself to the stepparent when I'm not home.
_____ Focusing on enjoyable activities with my stepchild.
_____ Using Problem Solving Skill to agree on house rules for everyone.
_____ Enforcing house rules evenly and fairly.
_____ Making 95% of my efforts with a stepchild on bonding experiences/ conversations.
_____ Allowing the bio-parent to deliver discipline to his/her bio-child.
_____ Allowing the bio-parent to be in charge of and make decisions about his/her child.
_____ Expecting my child to respond respectfully to the stepparent.
_____ Following through with natural, related consequences if respect is not given.
_____ Responding with Showing Understanding when any child expresses or demonstrates any feeling.
_____ Considering the input of the stepparent regarding my child when given respectfully and behind closed doors.
_____ Asking for a Skilled Discussion and Problem Solving regarding issues that involve the stepparent's well-being, time or attention.
_____ Being open to a perspective on my child that may have been a blind spot.
_____ Reacting calmly and finding appropriate, related consequences for broken rules.
_____ Spending more time reassuring and reinforcing my relationship with my bio- child.
_____ Spending special time with each bio-child.
_____ Looking for opportunities to give a special word of encouragement or acknowledgment to each child.
_____ Attending events that are important to each child, bio- or step.
_____ Noticing and encouraging the interests and abilities of each child.
_____ Honoring my spouses need to spend time alone with his/her bio-child.
_____ Taking a parenting class together. (Referral Information on page 83.)
_____ Giving the child a choice between two or more acceptable options.

Stumbling Blocks to Helping a Distressed Child:

_____ Reacting with anger or harsh punishment.
_____ Assuming the child will "get over it" in time.
_____ Ignoring or underestimating potentially dangerous behavior or aggressive tendencies.
_____ Ignoring continued withdrawal or loss of interest in favorite activities.
_____ Ignoring drastic changes in school work.
_____ Shaming, criticizing or telling him/her to "get over it."

Building Blocks to Helping a Distressed Child:

_____ Remaining consistent in expressing love *and* enforcing clear boundaries.
_____ Making sure the bio-parent does most of the interacting with the child.
_____ As a stepparent, remaining calm and supportive of the bio-parent and the child.
_____ As a stepparent, being patient and taking every opportunity to connect at the level of the child's interests.
_____ Being firm with safety issues.
_____ Looking for safe ways for the child to express aggression: sports, punching pillows, writing in a journal, talking with a neutral party.
_____ Looking for simple, natural consequences to misbehavior.

SUMMARY: No matter how deep your desire, there is no such thing as a perfect parent. Even trying to be perfect will guarantee that major mistakes will be made! I recently asked my adult son to name a few of the things I did as a parent that he remembers with gratitude. Here's his list: breakfast made every morning (except when I served papaya,) lunches packed, frequent trips to a nearby park, chocolate sheet cake, events with grandparents and extended family, camping trips, being his Little League team mom, birthdays, active church participation, a few Bible verses he still remembers memorizing, learning to ski, fishing with his great Uncle Don… Mostly simple things that only required that I be present and consistent. In spite of good memories, we still had some major hurts to work through from the early, chaotic stepfamily days. *And*, I had a lot of self-forgiveness to do for the ways I failed as a parent.

BUILDING TASKS:

Do the House Rules exercise with your current partner (found in Chapter Six) and enforce them consistently. Put only your most essential rules and consequences on the list. If you're unsure about the value of House Rules, watch the video at http://nancylandrum.com/stepping-twogether titled House Rules. Sherman and Alexa's experience will convince you that the effort is worth the results!

Active Parenting classes are available for all age level children and one program is particularly for stepfamilies. www.activeparenting.com to find a class near you.

Coming up…

Read how non-judgmental listening may be the prescription for healing your relationship to your child (or anyone else!)

CHAPTER ELEVEN: The Healing Power of Listening

Perhaps the most precious gift we can give our children is to deeply see them...to look into his eyes and allow that boy to see the pleasure felt by his simply existing in your life. To gather that little girl into your arms and convey with every fiber of your being that she is loved, no matter what! Read the following story about the incredible healing power of listening to your child without advice or judgment...

Big Bunny

by Robert Wolgemuth

John and his wife, Cindy, had been troubled by a growing emotional separation between themselves and their daughter Elizabeth. Elizabeth was getting further and further away from me, John confessed. Al thought I was losing my girl. Either she was making excuses for missing dinner or we were silently bumping into each other around the house. Our relationship was in a mess. The knot in my stomach was affecting everything in my life.

Late one evening he knocked on Elizabeth's door. John's daughter opened the door. "May I come in?" John asked.

Without a word, Elizabeth turned, walked back to her desk, and sat down, her back to her father. Assuming that it was okay to enter, John found a spot to sit on the corner of the bed.

"You know, Elizabeth," he began, "when I was a little kid I had a stuffed animal named Big Bunny."

The blank stare on Elizabeth's face as she turned to look at him let John know that his little story was not captivated her imagination and that he'd better get to the point.

"Whenever I was frustrated or scared or mad or nervous about something, I would talk to Big Bunny," John continued. "And do you know what? Big Bunny always listened to me," John said, feeling that old emotion as he remembered how he used to pour his heart out to his special stuffed friend. "I don't know what I would have done without Big Bunny."

After a lengthy silence, John finally said, "Elizabeth, I know you're growing up. You're a beautiful young woman And although it's been a long time since we put your stuffed animals away in the attic, I would like to give you a Big Bunny of your very own."

"Dad, you're not serious," Elizabeth said without hesitation, a tone of disbelief in her voice

"Don't worry," John said. "I know you're too old for an actual stuffed toy."

Elizabeth was visibly relieved.

He told her that whenever she wanted someone to talk to—someone who would not be critical; someone who would listen and not give advice—he would be her Big Bunny. All she had to say to her dad was, "Can I talk to Big Bunny?"

The ground rules were that John had to stop being dad. He could only listen. John could not criticize or give advice unless Elizabeth asked for it. Big Bunny was a free friend—not a coach, a teacher, or a minister...not even a parent! If Elizabeth's request came when John didn't have the time to listen, he would make an appointment with his daughter (for later...and keep it).

As John told me this story, his eyes filled with tears. "Big Bunny saved my life," he whispered. "Big Bunny is working. Elizabeth finally has a place to unload her frustrations and fears. Because of Big Bunny, our relationship is on the mend."

Taken from DADDY@WORK: Loving Your Family, Loving Your Job...Being Your Best in Both Worlds, by Robert Wolgemuth, p. 72-74. c. 1999 Robert D. Wolgemuth. Used by permission of Zondervan Publishing.

LESSONS FROM BIG BUNNY

When my children were little, I confess I thought it was more important for them to listen to me, than for me t listen to them! I thought I had the best answers for them...that they needed to hear and adopt my rules and wisdom.

My boys were adults before I learned the magic of listening to them...I learned how much respect I had for them, how much I loved their basic good characters and felt reassured that they had become men for whom I had a great deal of respect.

BE CURIOUS

Pay attention to what your child says or indicates as true for him/her. Ask, "Tell me what led you to that opinion..." Or, "I'm curious to know what you think of _____'s behavior. Do you feel like sharing that with me?"

Take these opportunities to learn about the formation of your child's thoughts...what influences his/her world? What is this child looking to for clues about how to be in this world? What is important to this precious being?

If you use these opportunities to criticize or convince your child to think more like you do, you're running the risk of that child simply hiding anything from you that doesn't meet your approval.

THE HARD PART

My late husband Jim used to say that parents tend to think of their children as extensions of themselves...their skills, intelligence, opinions, beliefs, morals, etc. But children do not think of themselves (at least in a Western culture) as extensions of the parents. Western children think of themselves as individuals with the right to choose beliefs and values that are unique to them. (My understanding is that in Asian cultures, children are more apt to be very conscious of their connection to the family...their importance to the family.)

Growing up is a process of trying on various roles or beliefs for size. Does this belief fit me? Is this the kind of man/woman I want to become? Do I just accept whatever I'm told by parents, teachers, friends, etc or do I want to think through what is true for me?

If we are carefully listening, we may hear some points of view from a child that are threatening or scary to us. Keep your cool. "Have you thought through what that belief may ultimately mean to you? Are you aware of what the consequences might be from this choice?"

As a game, or an experiment, try listening the way Big Bunny did...just caring and safe, no advice or criticism or attempts to steer this child's thinking into channels that feel safer to you.

What was it like for you to only listen? Temporarily step out of the role of parent, teacher, guide and just listen?

How did your child respond? Distrustful of your motives? More talkative, as though he was just waiting for the chance to share? What did you hear that surprised you?

On a scale of 1-10 with 10 being a great experience, what was this like for you? How do you think your child would rate this experience?

Are you ready to make non-judgmental listening a frequent part of your parenting? This is what happened when my client Chris recently tried Listening to Understand with his son...

> "Wow. Very enlightening. I have a child that gets frustrated easily, and I get frustrated with his frustrations. After a blow out on Sunday morning (he was very mad and crying and I was mad and hollering) I remembered that listening to understand may be useful to de-escalate arguments and solve misunderstandings. So I tried it...*I started acting like a grown-up again, and put aside my anger and frustration and asked my boy to tell me how he feels.* As he spoke, I repeated his words back to him. I just listened to what he had to say and made sure that he knew I heard him by repeating his words back to him. Slowly, but surely, he stopped his sobbing. As he talked, I continued to listen to understand and he continued to calm down. (I also continued to calm down!) After just a few minutes of listening to

understand I really felt much better and a lot more relaxed. I can't speak for my son's feelings after our short conversation, but and I'm pretty sure that he felt better too."

I suggested that a friend do this exercise with her ten-year-old daughter...

Repeat these questions over and over until the child can't think of another answer. Meet each answer with warm interest, but without comment or judgment:

What are you angry about? (answer) What else are you angry about? (answer,) etc, until the child can't think of anything else. Then,

What are you sad about? (answer) What else are you sad about? (answer.) Keep asking until the child can't think of anything else. Then,

What are you afraid of? (answer) What else are you afraid of? (answer.) Keep asking until the child can't think of anything else. Then,

What do you wish would change? (answer) What else do you wish would change? (answer) Keep asking until the child can't think of anything else. Then,

What are you grateful for (or happy about?) (answer) What else are you happy about? Answer...

During the sharing there were a few tears as the girl shared tender things. When they were finished and hugged, this precious child asked, "Mommie, can we do this exercise again sometime?"

This exercise is called *Taking Out the Trash*, used by permission by Richard Albertson, author of Adventures in Marriage curriculum. (www.LivetheLife.org) It works great for adults, as well. The important thing to remember is that you can't take any information you got from listening non-judgmentally and later use it against the person who so vulnerably shared! That would be a major violation of trust!

SUMMARY: Those who have learned to Listen to Understand (also known as Reflective Listening or Mirroring) have already experienced the amazing power of non-judgmental listening. The **Big Bunny** story does such a great job of illustrating how vitally important caring listening is in any relationship, but in this case, between a parent and a child.

Non-judgmental listening is the magic that creates emotional connection in any relationship. The deeper the respectful connection between parent and child the less need there is for rules and consequences.

BUILDING TASK:

Experiment with Listening for the Purpose of Understanding the world from your child's point of view. For the moment, discard your need to instruct, correct, warn or defend yourself. Just listen with caring.

COMING UP... How you can support your child's security by doing your best to successfully, respectfully co-parent with your Ex...

CHAPTER TWELVE: Making it Work for My Child

The Stepfamily Experience crosses all the ethnic, educational and financial strata of our world. This story may not represent circumstances that are familiar to you or your children. Yet, the circumstances that Michael experiences are similar to those of many children navigating through the maze following the breakup of his mother and father. Look for attitudes or actions of the adults around Michael for similarities your child may be experiencing.

NOTE: This exercise may be done individually or in a group. Whether reading this by yourself or using it as a group exercise, each listener gets a piece of paper and a roll of clear tape. Write IALAC in large letters on the paper. Whenever the story says "rip," tear off about a 2" x 3" piece of the paper. (Keep the torn pieces)

READER: This is a story about a boy named Michael and his journey from birth through age 15. When Michael was born, he came equipped with something called an IALAC sign. IALAC stands for "I am Loveable and Capable." Because it was invisible, no one—not his parents, relatives, or the doctor who delivered him knew it was there. In the earliest days of Michael's life when his young mother and father (who were happy and in love) stroked him, kissed him and admired him, his IALAC sign actually grew a little bit larger and stronger every day.

The IALAC sign is an indication that children come into this world free of self-doubt, feelings of shame, inferiority or anything negative. They must learn those things from the people and the world around them. And so it began for Michael.

Michael's parents were committed to each other and wanted very much to stay together as a family. Michael was a happy baby. At age four, Michael lived with his mom, dad and baby brother in a public housing complex. He enjoyed playing at the small playground in his complex. His dad would let him climb up to the top of the Jungle Gym, in spite of his mother's screams. It was fun! But as that year went by, Michael noticed that his mom and dad argued a lot. He covered his ears and cried whenever they started yelling. (Rip) Michael became nervous and irritable. (Rip) Pieces of Michael's IALAC sign began to crack and fall off.

Over the next year, Michael's dad started spending less time at home. Whenever he came home late, Michael's mom would yell at him. She would say things like, "I know you been out with some ho (whore)!" His dad would say, "No, I just want to get away from you!" Michael would get his little brother and hold him during the fights. He did it to help his little brother, but it helped him, too. (Rip)

One day when Michael was six, his dad moved out. His dad told him that he and his mom didn't love each other anymore...but they still loved him. Michael asked, "Dad, can you please stay here with us? Why don't you still love mom?" (Rip) His dad hugged him and said, "Sometimes things don't work out, son. Promise me you'll look out for your little brother because sometimes your mother just doesn't have good sense." Michael said he would, but something about that conversation made his stomach hurt. (Rip)

After his dad moved out, his mom talked to him a lot more. She told him her thoughts and feelings about all kinds of things. They were friends and Michael felt close to her. She talked to him about her boyfriend, Mr. Ron...and she also told him about things his father had done to her such as messing around with other women. One thing he didn't like was she asked him a lot of questions whenever he spent time with his dad. This made Michael nervous. He wasn't sure how to answer her questions. (Rip)

By the time Michael was 10, his mom was living with her new boyfriend, Mr. Tony, and his dad was living with Ms. Janice. Michael hadn't been seeing his dad much, but since he's been with Ms. Janice Michael spends a lot of time with them. His dad talks to him a lot more and helps him with his homework. His dad and Ms. Janice had a child, Shanice, his stepsister. When Shanice was born, everybody made such a fuss about her. It got on Michael's nerves...even now he thinks that Shanice is spoiled and gets all of his dad's and Ms. Janice's attention. His dad always has that little girl on his lap and his eyes light up when he sees her. (Rip) Michael has mixed feelings about Ms. Janice. Sometimes she's nice and sometimes she's mean. Yesterday, Michael's dad said he was going to marry Ms. Janice. It made Michael feel even more on the outside at his dad's house. (Rip)

When Michael told his mom that his dad was going to marry Ms. Janice, she got mad. Michael wished he'd kept his mouth shut. (Rip) They weren't as close now that Mr. Tony was living with them. Michael hated it when Mr. Tony kissed his mother in front of him...and when Tony told him to clean up his room or take out the trash. Tony wasn't his father! (Rip) But he did buy Michael a new video game system and played ball with him a lot.

One day Michael's mom called his dad's house to ask for some money. Ms. Janice answered the phone and his mother said, "Put Rick on the phone." Ms. Janice said, "That's so rude. Can't you even say hello?" Michael's mom said, "I don't have to say anything to you! This is none of your business!" Ms. Janice slammed the phone down. It was a mess. Both Ms. Janice and Michael's mom fussed about it for a week. (Rip)

By the time Michael was 15, he almost never saw his father. His dad said it was too hard trying to deal with his mother...but Michael could call him anytime he wanted. Michael didn't call much...he was too busy with his own life. He liked hanging out with two other friends, Ray and Anthony. They smoked weed together and it relaxed him. Michael had started having sex when he was 13 and was proud of it. Today he got suspended for having a tiny bit of weed in his locker. His mother was furious and told him he was just like his no-good father. Michael ignored her and turned the TV on...but inside he wondered, was he no good? Was he just like his father? (Rip)

READER: Instruct the participants to their best to scotch tape some of the IALOC pieces back together. By the time Michael was an adult, his IALAC sign had done a lot of mending. Young people are very resilient. But here were some pieces that were gone forever...[3]

Exercise by Mary Ortwein, MFW. Used in *Mastering the Mysteries of Stepfamilies* curriculum.

Lessons from Michael's Story

What did Michael's Dad do?

_____
_____
_____

What did Michael's Mom do? _____
_____

Look at the child's drawing of being torn between two parents. What may my child be feeling or experiencing?

_____
_____
_____

How did Michael respond?

_____
_____
_____

What does this story have to do with you? Check items that are true for you:

____Do we use our child to deliver messages?
____Do we use custody issues to punish each other? With our child caught between?
____Do I try to gain my child's approval by criticizing the other parent?
____Do I try to justify my decisions regarding that relationship by sharing inappropriate details?
____Do I acknowledge the difficulties for the child from the divorce?
____Do I criticize or run-down my Ex to or in front of our child?
____Do I brainstorm ways to make transitions between households easier with my child?
____Do I encourage phone calls, visits—contact—between our child and my Ex?
____Do my current partner and I recognize that the more we encourage the relationship with his/her other bio-parent the freer he/she will feel to accept my current partner and marriage?

Two good things I do now:

_____
_____

Two things I need to change:

_____
_____

Two things I will do to improve:

Stumbling Blocks to a Child's Successful Relationship to the Other Bio-Parent:

____ Using my child in a war with his/her other bio-parent.
____ Getting my child's loyalty and approval by criticizing his/her other parent.
____ Explaining what the other bio-parent did that caused the break-up of the relationship.
____ Fighting or escalating a fight in front of my child.
____ Criticizing my former spouse within my child's hearing.
____ Comparing my child's other bio-parent unfavorably with anyone else.

Building Blocks to a Child's Successful Relationship to the Other Bio-Parent:

____ Reminding myself often that a child will accept the stepparent easier if we both accept and encourage relationship with the other bio-parent.
____ Encouraging photos, notes, phone calls, visits with the other bio-parent if possible.
____ Talking about the other bio-parent with respect.
____ Acknowledging the importance of the other bio-parent to the child.
____ Listening with Understanding to my child's feelings about being separated, going back and forth between homes, or the loss of that relationship or parent.
____ Brainstorming with my child about how to make changes as easy as possible.
____ Practicing respectful speaking and listening skills with the other bio-parent.
____ Sparing my child the details or emotions of my former marriage.
____ Pointing out the strengths or abilities in the other bio-parent that I admire.
____ Carefully adhering to any agreements made in regard to custody and visits.

> In case you didn't see this quote before, *"Children can cope with two different homes and sets of rules if they don't have to choose which is best."* Elizabeth Einstein, Active Parenting

Stumbling Blocks to a Successful Parent/Other Bio-Parent Relationship:

____ Contributing to the escalation of upsets. (Keep your behavior respectful to de-escalate.)
____ Fostering verbal or emotional intimacies, such as talking to my former spouse about my current relationship frustrations or wins.
____ Using my child to deliver communications or dissatisfactions.
____ Sharing criticisms with my child about his/her other parent.
____ Telling my child unpleasant or inappropriate personal facts about the other parent.
____ Making my child choose which parent/home/set of rules is better.
____ Exposing the child to disagreements.

Building Blocks for a Successful Parent/Other Bio-Parent Relationship:

____ Working at building a cooperative parenting relationship by using good skills.
____ Making sure my romantic connections are broken/healed.
____ Forgiving and letting go of the past.
____ Using respectful communication skills in all interactions.
____ Using Showing Understanding to diffuse upsets.
____ Carefully keeping my agreements with my former spouse or those made by the court.

____ Using respectful notes to communicate if face to face interactions tend to deteriorate.
____ Setting up and using reliable methods of direct communication.
____ Writing down as much as possible rather than asking our child to relay messages.
____ Making sure events, issues or dates important to our child are communicated.
____ Asking the school to send duplicate notices/report cards or make copies.
____ Acknowledging anything good that I can about the other bio-parent.
____ Ensuring basic safety needs are met.
____ Ensuring our child is not exposed to inappropriate or dangerous behavior.
____ Settling disagreements apart from our child.
____ Doing all I can to foster a cooperative attitude with the other bio-parent.

Drafting a Co-Parenting Plan

Would you consider sitting down with your co-parent to draft a parenting plan? How do you think the other parent would feel about it?

What issues would you want spelled out in a parenting plan?

Use your good skills to dialogue about what you would like in a co-parenting plan with an Ex.

Repeating back what your co-parent says will help the expressing partner clarify thoughts. Using only respectful, calm language and tone with your Ex will help you both achieve the outcome that is best for your child.

You can't determine a co-parenting plan without the input of the co-parent, but you can think about what would be helpful.

If you already have a co-parenting plan, use the time to discuss any issues with the plan and how you might help it work better for your child's sake. Consider things over which you have control, rather than just wishing your Ex would change.

SUMMARY...

You'll find more help with letting go of limiting emotions (guilt, pity) and unhelpful behaviors (yelling, escalating arguments, blame) in the next chapter. Do your best to set aside your own agendas for the sake of meeting the needs of your child for two loving, cooperative parents who remain present and important in his life. Even if you can't do anything else right now, set a strong intention to do whatever it takes on your side of the relationship to give your child what she needs from her two parents.

BUILDING TASK:

Watch the video testimonials of James and Jeremy as each share what he learned about creating a workable parenting relationship with their respective Exes at http://nancylandrum.com/stepping-twogether

Coming up... How do I deal with my "crazy Ex" without going crazy myself?

CHAPTER THIRTEEN: The "Crazy" EX

So why is this chapter in the "nurturing a secure child" section of this book? Because, *to your child*, there is nothing more important than having the love and cooperative support from both biological parents. More than any other single element, this provides the climate for a child to feel secure and grow up with minimal wounds from the separation or divorce of their parents.

There are those amazingly mature and conscious divorced couples who do a wonderful job of co-parenting their children. I have enormous appreciation for a couple who is able to successfully let go of their former union and yet remain fully committed to responsibly meeting the needs of the child or children they share. If you and your Ex are seamlessly managing the co-parenting of your children, you may only read this chapter out of curiosity.

Some bio-parents resolve this issue by one parent basically dropping out of parenting, leaving the entire job of parenting to their Ex. Some in this category actually discontinue all contact with their child either because of disinterest, or because they mistakenly believe it is in the best interest of their child to reduce the confusion.

Also common, one parent becomes the "good time playmate" while the other parent carries the burden of "responsible" parenting. This is not only unfair to the "responsible" parent, but sets up a competition for the child's preference of parent that gives that child a warped view of what it means to be a good parent. When a child chooses the "good time" parent, that child probably is missing mentoring in adult life-skills that may set them up for unreasonable expectations about what life owes them.

For those who may fall into the more common patterns of continuing the issues with your former partner through the minefield of co-parenting, this chapter is for you.

TED and JULIE

TED: My legal battles to maintain joint custody of my two children have continued to this day. I've had to fight, through legal channels, to prevent my Ex from taking my daughter across the country to live. My Ex frequently comes up with new reasons to increase my child support which requires legal responses. I've gotten to know the court system so well that I frequently handle all but the most technical details without representation.

JULIE: We often attend the same sports or school events for Annie. At first, we would be careful to sit in a different location, or avoid getting close enough to converse. One day at a sports event I went up to TED's Ex and said, "You must be very proud of Annie. She's a lovely girl." The Ex was stunned into a civil response. It was a small thing to do, but may have helped the sense of rivalry over Annie that she seemed to encourage.

KIP and WENDY

Wendy: The thing I appreciate most about the work we've done is recognizing that *the kids come first*. We have to put aside our stuff in order to facilitate what is best for the kids...primarily in relationship to our former spouses. That piece has been huge in my relationship with Kip's boys.

We've worked so hard at it. I've had to put aside my emotional stuff and realize that it's more important for the boys to not have a loyalty conflict than for me to indulge in feelings of jealousy or resentment. It's huge. It's not jealousy in relationship to Kip. I'm certain I have his love and loyalty. *It might be more jealousy about the relationship she has with her sons. I want to be accepted and loved by his boys, too.* It means recognizing that there is that emotional piece that I must overcome for the sake of the children. I must move past my personal emotions and accept that for the next four hours or for this event I put aside whatever fears or anxieties I have to help the kids feel more comfortable. I'm even able to coordinate events with her for the boys, (such as birthday parties, etc.) Two of the boys have expressed their appreciation for my ability to co-operate with their mother. They don't have to choose between parents. We've worked so hard at this!

Kip: For me it's been a little bit different...a difference in personality, I guess. I just tried to go out of my way to say to Wendy's Ex, "Hi! How's it going?" I've encouraged Wendy to invite him to their children's birthday parties, etc. It's too bad that he really doesn't want to have anything to do with us at this point. He has a lot of things that he hasn't worked through, so he's uncomfortable. I've taken the active role of trying to help him feel more comfortable when we're all together.

Wendy: Kip is just a nice guy! It's more his nature to be a peacemaker, whether or not someone deserves it. When we were dating, I was getting along with my Ex and Kip was not getting along with his Ex. Somewhere in the process that flip-flopped. My Ex has been through two marriages since we divorced and for some reason that's left him in a place of not wanting to even be civil to me. He handles this by using our children to communicate with me. The children suffer because of that.

My oldest has very little to do with her dad. She doesn't want to hear what he has to say about me. She just doesn't want the conflict in her life. My son has almost nothing to do with him. My youngest sees him but it's very minimal...a couple of hours for dinner or something. It's miserable at his house and they don't want to be there. There is peace and caring in our house...a far more desirable place to be!

CHARLES and SUSAN

Charles: Susan's Ex is not a problem (for me.) He's irrelevant! He is his son's dad and I respect that tremendously, but he is not very involved in the activities or values that we have as a family. I'm sometimes frustrated that when they're at their dad's house they're not getting discipline, values or the school support I wish they'd get. But I don't have control of that. We have rules in this house! They'll figure out who did what for them as they grow up.

Susan: My relationship with my Ex is challenging! Our youngest is a type one diabetic. When you throw into the mix a child with special medical needs it adds to the challenges. His diet needs close management. There are doctor's appointments that require a lot of coordination. My Ex not communicative. It's very frustrating. I always have to initiate the communication. I lose my patience Charles helps bring me back to earth—be a voice of reason.

I have to repeatedly accept that it's not going to change. The responsibility falls entirely on us. I'm realizing that my children's life-skills must come from us. I just met my college son's roommate's father. He didn't know that I've been friends with the boy's mom for years. They have divorced and both remarried. The dad jokingly said, "I'm in charge of fun. CJ's mom is in charge of school, etc." That often seems to be the parenting pattern after a couple's divorce. It's hard to be the responsible one instead of the fun one!

JOHN and BESS

Bess: John's son Tim alternates weeks between our home and his mother's. There are changes every week. He has to adjust each time to different rules. His mother is an unseen member of our family. She alters the dynamic. His two households are HUGELY different! Nothing is similar! Even moral beliefs, lifestyles, rules, cities, environments…all are different. Consequently, Tim's personality is not easily congruent with our family dynamic. There is also John's guilt—his desire for Tim to be happy when he's here.

John: She nailed it!

HOW TO MANAGE A CRAZY EX (without becoming crazy yourself!)

There are two video interviews at www.nancylandrum.com on the **Stepping TwoGether** page where James and Jeremy each talk about the lessons learned in dealing with a volatile Ex. In the first year or two after their divorces, they both dished out as much as they got in reactive, explosive arguments. But it's significant that they each learned the same hard lesson…to simply (not easily, but simply) *not react* when their respective Exes were combative. They do not criticize their former Exes or get into a battle of who is (or was) right or wrong. They limit their interactions only to things that directly affect the children.

Jeremy refuses to reply to texts that are angry and abusive. Both men learned to keep their voices low and calm during any conversation requiring cooperation regarding their respective children. In both cases, the "crazy" Exes eventually (mostly) followed their lead and became more business-like and reasonable when it came to discussing issues regarding the children.

Others have found it helpful to delete abusive texts or emails rather than rereading them to "feed" their reactive anger.

It is highly recommended in the research that each spouse deal with his or her Ex. It frequently adds fuel to any issues doing a slow burn for the current spouse to get involved in discussions (or arguments) with the Ex of his or her partner.

That policy has worked well for all of the couples in our "cast." Lisa, Jeremy's wife, tried to be a voice of reason, intervening in issues between Jeremy and his Ex for the first few years. But then realized it only made things worse for her, and really didn't help to bring sanity for Jeremy or his children. Now she stays out of the fray, and gladly lets Jeremy handle any communication with his Ex.

From other couples I've heard that sometimes something as simple as waiting in the car for the children to arrive rather than going to the door to retrieve them will prevent harsh words or hurtful jabs.

I volunteer part time for our local police department. In cases where interaction with an Ex can possibly be unpleasant or even dangerous, the parents arrange to exchange a child in the lobby of the police department.

Get creative. Set boundaries. Learn to control yourself and accept that you can't control the other. Do whatever you have to in order to maintain as sane and respectful a relationship with your Ex that you possibly can. This is not only for your own emotional and physical health, but *for the sake of the children* who are wounded when their biological parents can't be civil, especially regarding the children's care.

MAKING IT WORK FOR MY CHILD'S SAKE

The Goal: To manage myself in a way that encourages a mutually respectful, cooperative relationship between me and my Ex for the sake of our child.

THE STRATEGY: As oxygen fans the flames of a fire, so impulsive, negative or disrespectful reactions cause exchanges to deteriorate. When clothing catches on fire the intuitive thing to do is to run. That's why many of us were drilled in the unnatural response of Stop! Drop! And Roll! If your relationship with your Ex has been characterized by anger or other forms of disrespect, a simple strategy is needed so that you can remember your goal when under the stress of an exchange.

"Stop!" Stop fanning the flames! All you have control over is your contribution to this relationship. *Respect is a chosen behavior* even when you may feel little respect for the other's behavior or character. (Review the communication methods listed at the end of **CHAPTER FOUR**. Each of those methods of communicating can be depended on to escalate an argument and make peaceful co-parenting much more difficult to achieve.)

Wait to vent your feelings away from your Ex and *never* in the presence of your child.

Resist the urge to retaliate. Stop the impulse to have a nasty retort or "the last word!"

Plan what you need to say ahead of time and stick to it!

Listen and repeat back what is said to reduce your Ex's strong emotions.

"Drop!" Drop every agenda except your goal to do what is best for your child.

Drop the need to retaliate, prove yourself right, blame or instruct.

"Roll!" Roll right into the respectful skills you've learned! (Again, See **CHAPTER FOUR**)

When discussing things concerning your child, listen with care to your Ex's thoughts, feelings, concerns and desires even though he/she may not be using good skills.

Repeat back (without "attitude") what is said to calm down upsets for the benefit of your child.

Plan what you need to say ahead of time using respectful speaking skills.

Stick to your plan...patiently repeating if necessary.

Follow through with agreed upon plans whether or not your Ex does!

COMMITMENTS: Check the ones you are ready to commit to do.

____ I choose to use good speaking and listening skills with my Ex for the sake of my own self-respect and the sake of my child.

____ I choose to be trustworthy in all my dealing with my Ex for the sake of my own self-respect and the sake of my child. ____ I choose to speak respectfully about my Ex to my child for the sake of my own self-respect and the sake of my child.

____ I will enlist the support of my spouse, a trusted friend and/or my faith community to help me keep these agreements.   ____ I will tell _____ about these commitments and ask for support.

> *Releasing myself from anger, guilt and blame gives me the freedom to make better decisions in the long-range best interests of my child. In addition, clearing away the emotional clutter makes it easier for me to commit my whole self to the success of my current marriage, my children and step-children.*

Choose the word you can accept most easily: ____ "Being at Peace" or ____ "Forgiveness." Place that word in the blanks below.

_____ is a gift I give myself and my child to release myself from the prison of hate.

_____ breaks the unhealthy bonds that may still attach me to my Ex.

_____ is for me and my child more than for the offender.

_____ can be given without trusting the other to change his/her behavior.

_____ can be embraced *and* take appropriate steps to protect myself and my child from disrespectful or abusive behavior.

_____ is a decision—a choice—not a feeling. I do not expect to feel differently right away.

_____ does not mean that I approve of or condone the other's behavior.

Whenever resentment or hatred arise for me, I will remind myself of my decision to _____. Gradually the angry or hurt feelings will lesson.

Stumbling Blocks to a Successful Parent/Other Bio-Parent Relationship:

____ Contributing to the escalation of upsets.
____ Fostering verbal or emotional intimacies, such as talking to my former spouse about my current relationship frustrations or wins.
____ Using my child to deliver communications or dissatisfactions.
____ Sharing criticisms with my child about his/her other parent.
____ Telling my child unpleasant or inappropriate personal facts about the other parent.
____ Making my child choose which parent/home/set of rules is better.
____ Exposing the child to disagreements.

Building Blocks for a Successful Parent/Other Bio-Parent Relationship:
Great quote: "Children can cope with two different homes and sets of rules if they don't have to choose which is best." (Elizabeth Einstein, Active Parenting for Stepfamilies.)

____ Working at building a cooperative parenting relationship by using good skills.
____ Making sure my romantic connections are broken/healed.
____ Forgiving and letting go of the past.
____ Using respectful communication skills in all interactions.
____ Using the skill of repeating back what your partner is saying to diffuse upsets.
____ Carefully keeping my agreements with my former spouse or those made by the court.
____ Using respectful notes to communicate if face to face interactions tend to deteriorate.
____ Setting up and using reliable methods of direct communication.
____ Writing down as much as possible rather than asking our child to relay messages.
____ Making sure events, issues or dates important to our child are communicated.
____ Asking the school to send duplicate notices/report cards or make copies.
____ Acknowledging anything good that I can about the other bio-parent.
____ Ensuring basic safety needs are met.
____ Ensuring our child is not exposed to inappropriate or dangerous behavior.
____ Settling disagreements apart from our child.
____ Doing all I can to foster a cooperative attitude with the other bio-parent.

SUMMARY: Controlling Your Behavior and Healing Your Own Wounds

There's no doubt it's a huge challenge to treat a "crazy" Ex with respect when they may not, in your mind, deserve respect.   It's even harder to forgive when the Ex hasn't acknowledged hurtful behavior or apologized. The challenge is to know that respect given and forgiveness of, or being at peace with the Ex is for your own mental health, the health of your new marriage, and even more, for the benefit of your child.

BUILDING TASK

Rehearse scenes where you maintain your cool, set a reasonable boundary (such as not responding to volatile texts,) and treat your Ex with respectful behavior. Ask for support when you need it. For instance, a good friend to go with you to a meeting with your Ex to give you the emotional support you need to maintain your intention to act in alignment with your values. (Best if this support is not your current partner!) Get whatever spiritual or counseling support you need to let go of anger and resentment and grief so that you can be at peace with the Ex whether or not he or she makes similar changes.

COMING UP...

How do you handle it when an adult child creates issues in your current marriage?

CHAPTER FOURTEEN: Parenting an Adult Child

Jim and I felt so much sorrow over our failure to recognize or adequately meet our children's needs during the traumatic upheaval in their lives created by our conflicts. We had been speaking about the healing of our SoulMate love for several years when a stepfamily support group asked us to speak about our experience as a stepfamily.

We said, "no" the first several times they asked, but finally agreed when they said, "Come and tell us what you did wrong." We bared our parenting souls and told them about all the hurtful things we did out of ignorance and blissful naiveté. By the time we found out that most step-families thrive with very different rules than biological families, and made some drastic changes, our children had suffered—some of them terribly.

In our defense, there were only a handful of books on the subject of stepfamily dynamics. Those brave authors were just beginning to expose the unique and, until recently, unrecognized foundational differences between a traditional, nuclear, biologically created family and a stepfamily.

One of the counselors we saw for a few visits was in a second marriage with "yours, mine, and ours." The therapist gave Jim some very valuable feedback about his relationship with Jimmy, but didn't have a clue about where I should fit in.

There's no doubt that both Jim and I loved our children every day of their lives and were *always* doing the best we knew how to do. Some of the mistakes we made definitely created pain for our children. But, parents cannot take full responsibility for the choices their adult children make. Each child is an individual with different tendencies, gifts, and potential flaws. A few of our children made choices we wouldn't have wished for them, going against the values we had modeled and taught...and suffered some painful consequences.

The bottom line is we weren't perfect persons or perfect as parents, then or now! Our kids weren't perfect either, then or now! The joy is that we eventually learned and grew together. Each of us has practiced forgiveness and acceptance so that today there is a lot of love, respect and even admiration between all of us!

You may have noticed in the interview snippets from each of the "cast couples" that difficulty in parenting is a repetitious theme. What hasn't been addressed until now is the hurt that may sometimes be caused by an adult child's reaction to a "new" family. Or, the residual wounds that may take time to heal. My boys were not openly opposed to my marriage to Jim, but the pain they experienced from the loss of my undivided attention on them took several years and many "Listening to Understand" sessions.

Jim had a beautiful baritone voice and was frequently asked to sing the national anthem at Angel baseball games. On one occasion it was the Los Angeles Lakers that scheduled him to sing for their game. I loved hearing Jim sing, but suggested that he invite three others to use the free tickets he got in exchange for singing.

I called my elder son Steven and asked if I could take him out for dinner. A little plaintively he said, "You mean you want to spend time with me? Instead of going to the Lakers game?" I said, "Yes!"

We had a lovely meal at a Mexican restaurant near his home. He talked non-stop through the whole meal. Although an adult, he still needed to know that he was important to me…important enough to pass up the chance to see Jim applauded at a Lakers game! There was a pang of pain in my heart as I realized he still had wounds from the mistakes I made during the beginning years of our marriage. At that time, I thought my biggest challenge was building relationships with my new husband and step-children. I didn't recognize that my birth children needed my reassurance more than ever before.

PARENTING ADULT BIO-CHILDREN

One middle aged couple called me for help. He had two grown daughters. Their mother had been living in a mental institution for many years before their dad divorced her. There was no possibility of her returning home. His new wife was a high school sweetheart. They reconnected at their 25-year reunion. She had no children and had never been married.

His daughters were acting out in pretty childish ways, like "accidently" spilling wine on the bride's dress and talking trash about her in her hearing. He thought the solution was to force all of them to spend more time together in order to know and like his new wife. What these daughters needed was to know they were still important to their dad. He arranged some visits with them, without the new wife, with two purposes: 1) to give them his full attention, reassuring them of how much he still loved them and wanted them in his life. And 2) Deliver a strong expectation that they treat his wife with courtesy. He said, "You don't have to like her. You don't have to approve of my marriage to her. But you must respect my choice and treat her with respect."

Soon the acting out calmed down.

In his single parenting, he'd done the best he could for them, but made some decisions based on his guilt about their missing mother. And like kids everywhere, they had learned how to manipulate his feelings to get what they wanted. Perhaps, he was far more generous and compliant toward them than may have been good for them. It was time for them to assume more responsibility for their own welfare rather than expecting Dad to always be exclusively at their beck and call.

This seems to be a common problem…

WEEDING OUT GUILT AND PITY

Another father called me after hearing me speak at a marriage support group. The "speech" that I deliver about every 13 weeks at this group is primarily about Jim's and my eventual policy of "respect 24/7" and how new communication skills saved our marriage. But I'm also transparent about the nature of our conflict being differences in our parenting of Jimmy and how we resolved that.

Tom and Mary (fictitious names) had been married about four years. He had three children. Mary believed that since she contributed to the financial balance sheet of the household, she should have a say about how much money went to the support of his adult children. Tom and Mary were fighting about money and adult kids.

Mary certainly deserved a "say" in how their combined incomes were spent. She needed to voice her opinion to Tom in a respectful way, but she took it further and, without Tom's agreement, took his adult daughter off of their cell phone and insurance contracts. *Not* good for the marriage!

Tom asked for a phone appointment with me to discuss this daughter, his wife and the issues.

Tom's daughter was hitting him where it really hurt, accusing him of not loving her anymore because he was cutting back on his financial support. This 21-year old daughter was making adult decisions such as moving across the country with her boyfriend, but she continued to play the "feel sorry for me because my mom died" card and the guilt card of "You're my father. You're supposed to take care of me!"

Naturally Tom wanted to be sympathetic to the reality that his daughter's beloved mother had died when she was twelve. And he desperately wanted to be a loving, good dad. The problem was that he was allowing the adult daughter to dictate his role as "loving father." If he didn't decide on and adhere to his own definition of loving father, this daughter would continue to manipulate his feelings in order to get relief from her adult responsibilities.

We talked about what it means to be a loving parent…how did he define it? He'd never tried to define it. I shared my opinion, "Being a loving, responsible parent means, to me, that you slowly guide the child toward the day when they can successfully be independent and self-reliant. In my opinion, if she's twenty-one and believes she's adult enough to quit school and move in with a boyfriend, then she's adult enough to get a job and pay her own phone and insurance bills."

Tom and Mary definitely need to work on their ability to be a team. Mary needs to let Tom deal with his own children. And Tom needs to stop making parenting decisions out of pity or fear that he's not "loving."

Expecting capable adult children to assume adult responsibilities *is loving* even if that child resents or even rails against your decision. There may be circumstances where parental help can be given, such as help with advanced schooling costs, or baby-sitting while their adult child earns a degree. But offering help is the parent's voluntary choice, not a choice that is the result of emotional blackmail. Not all help is forbidden! Only "help" that blocks an adult child from becoming appropriately self-reliant.

Other than the **How to Stay Married & Love It!** book, the book I am most proud of is **Pungent Boundaries.** That book is where I clarify the difference between age-appropriate expectations and "rescuing" a child (or someone else) from the natural consequences of his or her choices. Some rescuing actually cripples a child/adult from gaining confidence that only comes with being a responsible adult.

Pungent Boundaries shares my own journey of extricating myself from behaviors that were not healthy for me or my children. These behaviors are popularly known as co-dependence. The best definition of co-dependence I've ever heard is, "An imbalance of responsibility." One person assumes too much, or inappropriate responsibility while the other person in the relationship assumes too little responsibility.

Tom's daughter played the classic role of making adult choices that pleased her, but rejecting other less exciting adult responsibilities that would be appropriate for her to assume for her age and circumstances. Tom tended to be responsible for her expenses out of fear that it would be unloving to cut off her phone or insurance.

> **Parenting decisions motivated by Guilt, Pity or Fear rarely (or never!) result in healthy choices.**

As he heard the clear logic of my definition of a "loving parent," he knew he had to deal with his own fear of losing the relationship with his daughter if he insisted she be responsible for her adult needs.

POWERLESS ULTIMATUMS

Tom was good at announcing boundaries, ie, "Your phone bill is your responsibility after June 1st. You need to get a job to pay for it yourself." She promised to follow through. But then June 1st would come and go without any change.

Tom kept waiting for her to get a job...do what he knew she needed to do in order to pay for her expenses. *Tom couldn't control whether or not she got a job or paid for her own expenses.* He was trying to save himself from the pain of her anger and accusations rather than doing what he knew would help her "grow up."

Tom was missing a key element of a healthy boundary...the enforceable consequences. Boundaries are useless...impotent... without also stating and following through with consequences if the boundary is not honored. After our session, Tom agreed that he would give his daughter a specific date after which her name would be removed from their phone and insurance contracts. No more arguing. *No more giving of advice.* Just a simple, knowable result that would happen if she didn't arrange for her own contracts. *Tom could only control what he had control over*...taking her off of his contracts by a certain date that he made clear to his daughter. The daughter was then responsible for deciding how to pay for those services...or live without them.

Mary learned to let Tom make the tough choices regarding his daughter, and support his enforcement of the consequences. She gives her support by reassuring him that he is being very loving and responsible as a parent and comforting his insecurities.

Tom also learned to stop making Mary the "bad guy" in the family. He made it very clear to his daughter that this boundary and enforcement of it was entirely his decision.

MORE ABOUT GRIEF AND RESPONSIBILITY

Any loss, including divorce, needs to be grieved. And often grief is a process that takes time. Grief cycles around, hitting us at varied and unexpected times. A healthy response to grief is to acknowledge the loss and definitely allow the feelings...sadness, anger, frustration, helplessness, deep pain, the dreams of what life would be like if this loss hadn't been suffered.

An unhealthy response to grief is to turn it into a permanent reason why this grieving person deserves special favors. I'm not talking about occasional treats, or mercy given for an infraction. I'm talking about a pattern of making parenting decisions based on "feeling sorry for him/her."

Often the "feeling sorry for this child" really means, "I feel sorry for myself because I experienced this loss, also, and now I have to experience the additional pain of enforcing age-appropriate parenting decisions." It requires brave parenting to reflect on our deepest motives for whatever parenting decisions we make. Is this decision supporting age-appropriate responsibilities? Are the consequences of "disobedience" fitting for this offense and age-group?

When coping with demanding or out-of-control teens or adult children, you'll find sane, helpful support by attending Co-Dependents Anonymous meetings. The first visit or two may be a shock, so plan on attending at least six meetings before deciding whether or not CoDA meetings are for you. Contacts for groups in your area can be found in the phone book or online

SUMMARY:

Children of any age need to know they are loved and important to their parents. Of course. That is a given. And children of any age need to be responsible for behaviors appropriate for their age...and suffer the consequences if they drop the ball. Consequences are how many of us learn most of our life-lessons! Denying these valuable life-lessons from our children might be characterized as loving ourselves more than loving our child...caring more about relieving my own fears rather than allowing my child to learn lessons that are essential for his or her reaching successful adulthood.

BUILDING TASK:

What responsibilities would you list as appropriate for an adult to assume? How do you define "loving parent?" Is your child manipulating your guilt, fear, regrets in order to avoid assuming age-appropriate responsibilities? Will you consider that "taking care of things" for your child may be working against the ultimate goal of his or her functioning as a responsible adult? Do you need counsel from a neutral party in order to sort out your next steps?

COMING UP... What are my options as a step-parent? How does it work?

STEPPING TWOGETHER: BUILDING A STRONG STEPFAMILY

It may be unrealistic to expect instant connection and love with a step-child, but you can treat your step-child with courtesy and respect whether or not respect is given to you. Over time, there are things you can look for and do in order to build a caring relationship with your step-child

CHAPTER FIFTEEN: Step-Parenting

A former student, Kim, felt drawn to her young step-daughter Deanna and invested a lot of time and energy into building a good relationship with her. When, as a result of the birth mother's jealousy, Deanna chose to end the close relationship with her step-mother, Kim was crushed. Because Kim was so much more emotionally stable than the birth mother, Kim made a typical stepfamily assumption that she, with caring and compassion, would command the loyalty due a real mother.

Other step-parents I've talked with report the pain when they face the unrealistic expectation that they will be a real grandparent to their step-child's children.

One father with whom I spoke didn't protest when his bio-son called his step-father "Daddy" because it was less confusing for the boy. What an amazing sacrifice in service to the welfare of his son!

There are wonderful exceptions to these experiences, but the relegation of a step-parent to a much lower rung on the *real family* ladder is more often the truth.

Read this true story about a step-father's journey toward building a caring bond with his step-daughter. Answer the questions following the story as truthfully as you can.

OUR BOOK BOND

by Ptolemy Tompkins

Senior Contributing Editor, Guideposts Magazine.

September, 2008 Issue

I moved into my new wife Rebecca's Greenwich Village apartment back in 1994, and knew that it would take a while before I really felt at home. Like most New York apartments, Rebecca's was small. It was also crammed full of her and her seven-year-old daughter Mara's stuff. Where, in this jumble of Fisher-Price toys, leotards, record albums and Polly Pocket lunch boxes, would I fit any of my stuff?

Most important, my books. Ever since I was a kid, I've been one of those people who doesn't just read books. I arrange my life around them.

Not that there weren't plenty of books in the apartment already. Most of the wall space was taken up with Rebecca's bookshelves. And Mara's little bedroom was packed with them too. Apparently, Mara was a reader just like her mother.

It was the one tenuous connection I felt with her. Though Mara was polite, I could tell I was basically just another alien adult in her eyes.

Mara was a very different kid than I had been. I had been quiet, dreamy, solitary...much happier with my head buried in a dinosaur book than with a bunch of other kids my age. Books were my friends. Mara, on the other hand, was intensely social. She did her reading in between visits to friends' houses and very long chats on the telephone.

Even the books that Mara read were hard for me to figure out. One day not long after I moved in, I pulled out the paperback that was poking from the top of her backpack and gave it a quick examination: *Sideways Stories from Wayside School*, by someone named Louis Sachar. Glancing at the back cover, I divined that it was about an elementary school that had been built sideways, and the adventures of the school kids who went there.

It was the last kind of book I would've been interested in at her age. Too many characters. Too much dialogue. No dinosaurs. No sharks. What kid would want to read that?

But from that day on, I studied the covers of the books she toted around and tried to get the hang of which ones appealed to her and which ones didn't. Most books got just a single reading. But when Mara really liked a book, she returned to it again and again, bringing it with her to school, to bed...even into the tub. I had felt the very same way about my favorite books when I was her age.

"There's some free shelf space out on the sun porch," Rebecca said to me one afternoon. "Why don't you get some of your books out of storage and set them up there?" With each book I pulled out of the boxes, I felt more at home—more like this wasn't just where Mara and her mom lived, but where I lived, as well.

One day at Barnes & Noble I dipped into the kid's section and picked up a few titles for Mara. "Thanks!" she said when I handed them over. Sure enough, one of them was a volume called *My Crazy Cousin Courtney* that looked like it had Mara written all over it started showing up again and again around the apartment. I'd scored a hit!

From then on, I bought Mara books regularly—and not just from Barnes & Noble, but from rummage sales and flea markets too. With each one, I got to know her just a little bit better and came closer to feeling like I might really belong in her life after all.

One June day when Mara was fourteen years old, I came home and found a square package on the coffee table. "What's that?" I asked Rebecca.

"Why don't you open it and find out?"

It's hard to buy me books. Especially on subjects I like. But the one in that package—a big pictorial natural history of sharks—was one I'd never seen before. "For Ptolemy," read the inscription. "Happy Father's Day, with love from Mara."

Books are funny things. They just have a way of making you feel at home.

What can be learned from this story? What did Ptolemy do?

___

What did Ptolemy not do?

___

What character traits did Ptolemy demonstrate?

___

How long was it before Mara gave him a "Father's Day" gift?

___

What behaviors, attitudes or expectations might you duplicate?

___

How can you begin to put these plans into practice?

___

Like constructing a building, a caring step-relationship requires long-term planning and commitment. Quick results are the exception, not the rule.

Stepparent: A Tough Role—Some Tough Questions

What is hardest for you about being a step-parent?___

What kind of relationship do you want? (Name at least three qualities of the relationship you want.)
___

Do you wish you could have the marriage but not the responsibility of a step- parent?___

Do you want to be treated like *the real* parent?___

Do you want control over parenting decisions? Or think you can do a better job parenting than your partner or the other bio-parent?___

Do you resent that your partner doesn't accept your suggestions about parenting this child?
___

What do you want from this child?_____

Do you feel in competition with the step-child's bio-parent? Do you need this child to believe that you are better than their bio-parent?_____

Do you need this child's approval?_____

Do you feel resentment for the time and attention your partner gives to this child?_____

Do you experience hurt feelings when your partner spends one-on-one time with his/her child? Or when the child rejects you?_____

Will you need to function like a nuclear family before you feel successful?_____

Do you find yourself taking your frustrations out on this child? Or blaming this child for the issues with your partner?_____

Describe how you wish it could be:
_____
_____
_____

It's easy to answer these questions the way you think is *the right answer*, but in the days and weeks ahead, when upsets happen inside you or between you, your partner and/or your step-child, review these questions and ask yourself, "Could this expectation be causing this upset? What do I need to adjust?"

Stumbling Blocks to a Successful Stepparent/Stepchild Bond:

- ____ Competing for the child's affection or loyalty with either bio-parent.
- ____ Expecting or demanding love.
- ____ Trying to force a close relationship with the child.
- ____ Saying "I love you" too soon. (It may feel false and uncomfortable to the child.)
- ____ Taking it personally when my stepchild ignores or rejects my efforts.
- ____ Allowing discouragement to stop my efforts.
- ____ Expecting perfection.
- ____ Indulging in expressions of anger at my step-child.
- ____ Criticizing or comparing one child with another.
- ____ Criticizing my spouse or the child's other bio-parent.
- ____ Trying to take the place of the missing parent.
- ____ Expecting to be acknowledged on holidays.
- ____ Expecting to be honored at special events.
- ____ Expecting to be the grandparent of my step-child's children.

Building Blocks to a Successful Stepparent/Stepchild Bond:

- ____ Having reasonable expectations. This is not a "first" family relationship!
- ____ Accepting that the bonds with my stepchild will rarely be as strong as to my own child.
- ____ Making caring, respect and trust my goals.
- ____ Accepting the importance to the child of both bio-parents.
- ____ Encouraging the relationship between the child and other bio-parent.

____ Noticing the stepchild's interests and abilities. Be his/her cheerleader.
____ Looking for opportunities to encourage and/or praise for specific things.
____ Paying attention to events that are important to the child.
____ Offering to teach a skill.
____ Writing occasional notes of appreciation for progress in attitude or accomplishment.
____ Respecting my stepchild's privacy by always knocking and waiting to be invited in.
____ Showing Understanding whenever feelings are expressed. Showing Understanding!
____ Asking for a Skilled Discussion with my spouse when a stepchild is disrespectful.
____ Acknowledging the difficulty of changing traditions and habits.
____ Praising whatever you can about both bio-parents.
____ Being very patient!
____ Being patient! VERY

> **TRUTH: The more you encourage your step-child's relationship with both bio-parents, the faster that step-child will accept you.**

Please read the above statement again! There it describes a powerful truth that can make your relationship with your step-child evolve much more smoothly!

There are definitely some challenging roles and relationships to be juggled in a stepfamily! When a step-parent has an unequal role in parenting it is particularly critical that both adults are honest and realistic in their expectations from each other in relationship to the child. There are some very real payoffs and benefits that come with having less responsibility for your step-child.

> **Julie:** When we adhered to the policy of *no commenting or criticizing of each other's children or parenting decisions,* it was like a magic pill had been dropped into our home. The fighting immediately stopped." And, "Our children are living with a model of a healthy marriage for the first time in their lives. Ted and I are absolutely sure now that we will stay together and love each other until parted by death! It feels indescribably safe to have that security!"

> **Ted:** As we and the children feel more secure, layers of issues are surfacing that require us to continue using our skills and stepfamily guidelines. We're doing a better job of listening to our children. Now that we're not busy being defensive with each other about our parenting, we're becoming more attentive to the needs of our children.

> **Wendy:** We've raised our children differently. We have different personality types and temperaments. To try to 'blend' our kids and our styles was not practical. Kip's strength is grace. He's able to look past things I would find offensive. I'm more structured, disciplined. Over time I observed that there's strength in his grace and he's seen that there are areas where he needs to step up and be more firm on certain issues. We've worked out a balance. But most importantly, we each discipline our own children.

> **Nancy,** "…when I relinquished my role as traditional mom to Jimmy…I no longer had the responsibility of trying to figure out what was best for (him). A huge source of conflict was eliminated between Jim and me. And, any problem Jimmy might have could no longer be blamed on me."

Jim defined his role to my boys as a "kindly uncle." He didn't force himself on either Steve or Pete, but offered what he wanted to offer when an opportunity arose. For instance, he took Peter out to practice his driving skills. He and Steve enjoyed watching boxing matches together. In time, both boys enjoyed chatting with Jim. Jim's relationship with my boys grew organically over time. Both boys, by the time they were men, expressed affection and great respect for Jim.

Charles: Some fathers want to be liked by their kids. The father treats them as a friend, rather than being a father. I think Susan's Ex is insecure. He's had multiple relationship failures. His second wife also left him because he couldn't stay committed. The boys love him so much. That's understandable, but he lets them do whatever they want to do. My fear is that they think this is what a father is. My challenge is to model more responsible behavior. Eventually they will choose the kind of men they will be. I model respect toward women. I model commitment. I demonstrate that I work through the difficult things in life. If they choose those qualities for themselves, then I've been a good stepfather.

What payoffs, benefits or outcomes can you imagine if you adopt these stepfamily strategies?
_____
_____
_____

There is little doubt that being a stepparent is sometimes a thankless job. It requires flexibility and almost limitless patience. The experience of being under the same roof with a child or children over whom you have limited control and little say in decisions concerning them is a challenging condition for most adults.

The mind-set that makes this so hard is often the pre-conceived ideas a stepparent brings into the family. We've spent a lot of time emphasizing the need for a new paradigm for "family" when it comes to stepfamily relationship guidelines. The shift from a "first family" mind-set to a stepfamily mind-set can be painful. In my personal experience, it was excruciating for me to give up my "right" to give Jim my great parenting advice in regard to his children. It didn't seem to occur to me at first that I didn't have a perfect track record as a parent, either! I was sure I was *right* about what Jim's kids needed from him! I've learned since that this is an almost universal stance by stepparents! A stepparent doesn't look through the rosy lens created by the millions of sweet interactions a parent enjoys with their bio-child from inception on.

Since then I've grown to appreciate how valuable that rosy lens is! It often keeps parents from being overly harsh or have excessively unreasonable expectations for a child. Of course, this blurred condition also means that some parents err on the side of being too permissive or blind to the long-term consequences of a child's behavior.

The situation can be further complicated if you, the stepparent, charges in expecting to be loved, to be appreciated as the great role model that the other bio-parent isn't or trying to "rescue" the spouse from an unruly child. Also, if the expectation is that "finally I'll have the family I've wanted" there is bound to be disillusionment!

Some rare and amazingly mature stepparents come into this role without any need to compete with the other bio-parent or prove themselves as wonderful to their new spouse or the stepchildren! When that is true, the situation is simplified considerably, even though it may still be challenging.

For those who enter the family with "unrealistic expectations" as well as being opinionated and sure that your spouse needs your help, the process of adopting a more mature, workable, realistic role can be a crash course in personal growth! A good thing, ultimately, but wrenchingly painful in the process.

Another reaction can be relief! You may be glad you can turn the primary responsibility over to the bio-parents and just want some coaching about how to be supportive.

All of these reactions and conditions require patience and empathy for both the parent and the stepparent...not to mention the children! A stepfamily, like a first family, is a living organism that is in a constant state of growth and adjustment. You deserve high commendation for being open to new information.

GRADUATED PARENTING

Graduated Parenting is the term applied to the following concept: Over years, the stepparent may or may not gradually begin to meld into a more traditional parental role. The younger the child, the sooner the stepparent may be able to assume a semi-parental role, with the approval of the biological parent. If you want to develop a caring relationship with your step-child, your first priority is to watch for opportunities for bonding with the child by showing interest in that child's interests. The child is ultimately in charge of how fast those efforts will be accepted. With some children it's almost immediate. With others a bond develops over many years—or never. The stepparent only assumes a more traditional role of authority/parent as the relationship with the child builds. A general rule of thumb is that it takes up to the same number of years to be fully accepted by the step-child as the age of the child when the marriage took place.

It is so important to be truthful with your partner about what works for you and what doesn't. It's also important to remember that you knew your partner had children when you agreed to this marriage. Now that you're committed to the love-relationship with your partner, it's only fair to also commit to whatever is needed in terms of your partner's responsibilities to his or her children.

SUMMARY: Decide on what role you wish to play in the life of this step-child. Start off slow and easy. If you wish to develop a caring relationship, begin by just watching, observing, noticing the interests of this child. How can you share that interest? Contribute to it? Can you offer help or caring questions without being offended if your offering is met with coolness or even rejection to begin with? Are you willing to support (without criticism) the bio-parenting decisions regarding this child? What do you need from your partner in order to be content in this family? Have you done the **House Rules** exercise with your partner? What are the basic minimum behavior requirements you need from your step-child? Are you and your partner in agreement about House Rules and your freedom to enforce the consequences?

BUILDING TASKS:

Decide what role you are willing to play in your step-child's life. Work out the details with your partner. Get a power of attorney signed so you can authorize medical treatment if there's an emergency.

Coming Up...   Making your stepfamily safe for all...

Important note: The stepparent has no legal authority to authorize emergency medical help, sign field trip permission forms, get confidential information from the school, etc.

____   Print out a copy of a Limited Power of Attorney to authorize medical treatment for my stepchild.

____   Keep copies in places easy to find in an emergency (wallet, glove compartment of the car, etc).

Power of Attorney:

A Power of Attorney is a document under which you as the "Principal," give legal permission to another person or entity (an "Attorney-in-Fact" or "Agent") to act on your behalf. You sign a Power of Attorney document so that your Agent will be able to handle your affairs during a period of time when you are unavailable or unable to do so. An Agent is not required to be a lawyer.

A Power of Attorney may be either general or specific. A General Power of Attorney gives the Agent broad authority to act for you. A Special Power of Attorney grants the Agent limited authority to act only in specified situations. In addition, you may create a "Durable" Power of Attorney, which means it will remain in effect even if you become incompetent or incapable of handling your affairs. If you do not want the Power of Attorney to remain in effect during these times, then the document can be made "non-durable."

Note: A separate Power of Attorney should be created for each person, each child. A "joint" Power of Attorney is not valid.

When you search "free power of attorney form," several options come up. Choose one that is recognized in your state. One option is at: www.LawDepot.com

CHAPTER SIXTEEN: Creating Safe Boundaries

This may be an uncomfortable topic for some. I would be irresponsible, however, if I ignored the issue of abuse in stepfamilies.

Abuse happens in all kinds of families, but statistically is more prevalent in stepfamilies, and happens even more often in cohabiting families.

Women tend to deliver more Verbal and Emotional abuse. Physical and Sexual abuse more frequently happens from men. At a national marriage conference, I heard a presentation where it was pointed out that we enact laws against physical and sexual abuse, usually associated with men. And those laws are very appropriate. I only wish the penalties were greater! But women may create as much emotional and psychological damage with harsh, judgmental words. We tend to underestimate how profound the damage can be from verbal and emotional abuse.

WHY?

So why should the structure of a step- or cohabiting family produce more abuse? There are two main reasons cited.

The first is hardly a surprise. Higher levels of stress have been connected with higher levels of abuse of all types.[4] As you learned in CHAPTER ONE, stepfamilies have significantly higher levels of a stress than first families.

The second reason is that there is sometimes a less caring connection in step-relationships. Elizabeth Einstein describes this well in the Stepfamily Bonding Triangle.[5]

There are three strong bonds between a biological parent and child, represented by three lines. Those are:

- Biological. They share the same DNA and that parent Has been present for that child since its inception. For emotionally healthy birth-parents, it's a powerful bond. For centuries, the biological bond trumps nearly every Other kind of relationship possibility.
- Emotional. This parent has literally thousands of emotionally bonding interactions with child, beginning in utero, then birth, then feeding, caring for and watching for every proof of physical and emotional progress. The first smile. The first steps. The first word…and on and on. Every exciting moment of development, every moment of caring for a sick child, strengthens the emotional bond.

Justice & Justice, 1976: Straus, et al., 1980
Copyright 2007 by Active Parenting Publishers. Used with permission.

- Legal. It is mandated by law that a parent provide food, shelter, clothing, education and safety for their biological child. When those things are not given, Child Protective Services can remove the child from the parent and see that it's needs are met by a surrogate or foster parent.

The bonds between the parent and step-parent are compelling, as well, represented by two lines:

- In our culture, the couple commit to share life together because of a strong emotional bond we call "falling in love." There is usually strong sexual attraction and mutually given sexual satisfaction that deepen the emotional bond. Those emotions lead to the belief that "We belong together. We can do this. I can't live without you."
- Marriage is a legal contract as well. Some have painfully learned that each partner shares in the responsibility for repaying the debts assumed by the other. The law assumes that if one dies, the other inherits the deceased partner's assets.

In contrast to the three bonds of parent and child, and the two bonds between parent and step-parent, the bonds between a step-parent and the step-child are represented by a dotted line. The relationship is

- New, and consequently
- More fragile.

The fragile bond between a step-parent and step-child in combination with more stress in a stepfamily, provide the breeding ground for abusive behaviors. The step-parent doesn't have the millions of bonding moments that tend to temper or reduce excessive over-reactions against a biological child. Biological parents can be abusive to their own children, but the incidents rise dramatically in a step- or cohabiting family.

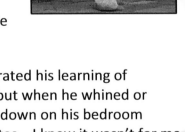

JIM and NANCY

> **Nancy:** Even though I wasn't aware of how much more my boys needed from me during the early years of my marriage to Jim, I had years of precious memories and bonding experiences with them that made it possible for me to see beyond their acting out behaviors. Jim had no history with them, so was impatient and offended by one's rudeness and the other's defiance. He was seeing them for the first time at their worst.
>
> I had not given birth to Jimmy; had not watched him learn to walk or celebrated his learning of language. When he shared some boyish treasure with me, I was touched, but when he whined or pestered, I was annoyed. I felt guilty and helpless one night when he, face down on his bedroom carpet, wailed, "I want my Mommy!" over and over for at least thirty minutes. I knew it wasn't for me his little broken heart was crying.

As the step-parent, we have no history and no bonding from which to draw tolerance or to temper our irritation. It is so classic as to be a rule that the step-parent sees what the stepchild needs more clearly than the biological parent. Children were meant to be reared by biological parents for this very reason…the "rules" are softened by the loving bond. That bond, at least in the beginning, is absent in the step-relationship.

This explains why a step-parent may believe the step-child needs more structure...more discipline...more control...prompting parent-like actions that offend the bio-parent and create resistance/rebellion in the step-child.

One step-father saw, and wanted to correct, behaviors in his step-son but was completely blind to very similar behaviors in his biological children. His children were "fine." Her child needed more discipline. His hard line and caustic, frequent criticism of the boy eventually caused the marriage to fail.

Another step-father of my acquaintance would not go beyond the doorway into his step-daughters' rooms. He knew that both of them had been sexually abused by their biological father. He made the physical boundary between himself and the girls very clear and definite. He did not want them to have any apprehension about sharing a home with him and their mother.

> THE GREATER MY CAPACITY TO *BE* THE OTHER PERSON, (EMPATHY) TO SEE THE WORLD THROUGH HIS OR HER EYES, THE MORE I WILL CHOOSE SAFE, COMFORTABLE AND RESPECTFUL BOUNDARIES.

The need for healthy boundaries is not only true for the step-parent, but for step-siblings, as well.

KIP and WENDY

Wendy: We definitely have been aware of potential issues between our respective teens! Our two youngest have a lot of the same friends from church and school. There's been some match-making! My daughter enjoys having her friends pair up so she's actually set up dates for Greg. We've talked with them about appropriate dress around the house. They responded with "Oh, Mom! Oh, Dad! We're just brother and sister! Nothing's going to happen!" But we know the statistics and the realities about step-sibling relationships so we make sure that they're never home alone together for too long. When Kip was a single dad, he and the boys were pretty casual about walking around in jockey shorts, etc. That doesn't happen now! We've had no issues that we've actually had to face, but we're aware of the possibilities and keep our eyes open rather than being in denial about the fact that something potentially damaging *could* happen.

Kip: We just use common sense. (Common sense to them, but not to everyone. If you have any questions, consult a professional.)

Wendy: Although Greg is here about half of the time, he's never had a room of his own so he's often slept on the couch. He tends to dress down for bed! He realizes that until he has a room of his own, when he's sleeping in a "public" space, he needs to dress appropriately. He can't go to the bathroom in his boxers! Although we're family, we do not share the same biology. There are some things that are appropriate and some things that aren't. Kip's family was four boys. The boundaries were different for them to begin with than in my family with a boy and two girls. We had to work on that a little bit but there weren't any major issues about it.

BOUNDARY SUGGESTIONS

1. Knock and get permission before entering another's bedroom or bathroom.
2. Modest clothing for both adults and children.

3. No affection that creates discomfort for the receiver or observer.
4. Bathing and dressing are private events.
5. Limit wrestling or horse-play where one is physically dominant over another.
6. Listen to your child/step-child if there are complaints about being hurt or uncomfortable.
7. Make house rules that respect everyone's personal space and belongings.
8. Ask questions and respect the answers, such as, "Would you rather your mom/dad help you with this?" "Are you comfortable with _____ or would you rather _____?"
9. Your Master Bedroom should have a lock...and use the lock. Children should not be able to walk in to your bedroom unannounced or uninvited.

Non-related persons living in the same space require more care around issues of clothing, privacy and sexual behavior. Modeling respect for a child's personal boundaries teaches, "I have the right to be treated with respect by everyone." Allowing a child to speak up when he/she is uncomfortable teaches, "It's O.K. for me to say 'No' when I'm uncomfortable."

HIGHLY RECOMMENDED

It is recommended by all step-family experts that older step-siblings not be entrusted with the care of younger step-siblings unless or until you are very sure a safe, caring bond has been created between them.

THE ANTIDOTES

The same skills that build and protect the marriage also protect the children in your stepfamily.

> **More Skills, More Peace = Less Stress, Less Abuse**

Verbal Abuse is eliminated or greatly reduced by learning and using respectful speaking skills with *everyone*.

Emotional Abuse is eliminated by practicing empathy (Listening to Understand) with, not only with your partner, but his/her/your children.

Physical and Sexual Abuses are eliminated by healthy anger management and effective problem solving. In *most* cases, the previous statement is true. But if there is a predilection toward violent anger or sexual attraction toward children, that person needs to get professional help in order to protect the child/ren in the family. The adult needs to believe what a child may tell him/her about sexual or physical acts that cause the child hurt or emotional discomfort. Although I have hated to do so, I've recommended that a spouse with violent anger or a sexual attraction to a child be removed from the home. The safety of the child/ren must come first!

HONEYMOON BEHAVIOR

In the stepfamily world, we laughingly say that step-couples get a honeymoon years after the wedding...when the children are grown and gone! When your relationship is new, exciting and filled with sexual energy, it's important to have boundaries about how overtly sexual you are in front of your children. Hugs, non-passionate kisses, temperate cuddling while watching T.V. are gestures of affection that should be comfortable...and even reassuring to most children. But anything that smacks of foreplay needs to be reserved for when you are alone or bedroom time!

Children love to know that the adult caretakers in their lives love each other. It's reassuring that *this* relationship is providing them the secure environment they need in order to thrive. But children, particularly adolescent and teenage children do not need to be exposed to highly sexual energy between you!

SUMMARY

Good, healthy boundaries provide emotional and physical safety and comfort for everyone in the family. Stepfamilies in particular need to be aware of the possibility of verbal, emotional, physical and sexual abuse and set boundaries around their own, and the siblings' behavior to prevent abuse.

BUILDING TASK

Tackle the tough topic of abuse with your partner. Be open to feedback from each other about possible verbal or emotional abuse. Learning to speak and listen with respect are skills that not only benefit and strengthen your marriage, but every other relationship, as well. Setting and enforcing boundaries that protect each person's privacy and safety is one of the tasks of leading a stepfamily. Seek knowledgeable, professional help if there is any question of abuse.

Coming up... More examples and wisdom from The Cast...

STEPPING TWOGETHER: BUILDING A STRONG STEPFAMILY

This section includes things that didn't fit in the other sections... More wisdom from The Cast, profound sharing from two step-kids, and seeing your stepfamily as an on-going process.

CHAPTER SEVENTEEN: More From The Cast

Parts of the original interviews were not used in the rest of this book, but have valuable tidbits of information that you may find helpful. In addition, I've added recent updates for a few of the couples. These couples' stories have added so much breadth and practical wisdom to the general topic of "stepfamilies."

TED AND JULIE:

Ted: Right after the class we thought everything was fixed, but in the months since then we've realized that a lot of damage was done during all the chaotic years. Now we are taking things one step at a time. As we and the children feel more secure, layers of issues are surfacing that require us to continue using our skills and stepfamily guidelines. We're doing a better job of listening to our children. Now that we're not busy being defensive with each other about our parenting, we're becoming more attentive to the needs of our children. We're more realistic about the fact that our stepfamily issues will continue to be a challenge, probably for the rest of our lives. Our children will continue to need our love and support as they move into adulthood with the wounds from their childhoods. We hope that they will follow our lead by learning these (communication) skills to make their first and only marriage succeed. We pray that they will stop the legacy of divorce with all its pain and chaos that Julie and I have handed them.

Julie: The great news is that the kids are living with a model of a healthy marriage for the first time in their lives! Ted and I are absolutely sure now that we will stay together and love each other until parted by death! It feels indescribably safe to have that security!

Ted: We are committed to helping other stepfamilies find the miracle we are experiencing. We recently co-taught a class with Nancy where couples thanked us for sharing our story! We are sharing our story anywhere asked and with anyone who will listen. Even relationships with our extended families are being healed. Finally, we are seeing some positive purpose for all the years of pain and misery. We are not only giving our children a safe, loving, respectful home environment but are helping other hurting stepfamilies find what they were searching for when they married. We are richly and truly blessed.

Recent Update: For Father's Day last year, Ted received a letter from his early-twenties step-son thanking him for the work he saw Ted do to learn how to love Julie better and for the changes he made in order to preserve their floundering stepfamily. After being abandoned by his birth father and his first step-father, for the first time in this young man's life, he had an example of a loving, sacrificing, caring man.

Ted and Julie are still in love and doing a great job of working through some difficult circumstances as a committed team.

KEN and IRMA

Ken and Irma attended my *Mastering the Mysteries of Stepfamilies* course as participants and then co-taught that curriculum with me. Currently they lead a non-profit support group for couples in distress (*The Third Option,* a national program) and teach marriage retreats for couples who want more from their marriage.

CHARLES AND MARY:

How was it to have four teens in a relatively new stepfamily?

> *Charles:* Not easy. It wasn't quite like commanding a battalion in combat, but close. When we got married we knew that we would have to do some work. We'd thought about *some* things. Hindsight being 20/20 I'd say that it's impossible to anticipate how much work it's going to be. It takes a tremendous amount of effort! Having some knowledge ahead of time would help, but we did "discovery learning"—meaning we discovered what we needed to learn as we went along.

What has surprised you?

> *Mary*: I've been surprised that some of the relationships are the opposite of what I expected in the beginning. Eileen was the least open to me…the most resistant. Madelyn and I hit it off in the beginning—shopping, arts and crafts, etc. Now Madelyn's the least open to the stepfamily. *Everyone's* gone through the journey in a way I didn't expect. One has sought the help of a therapist for grieving and adjustment issues. The other hasn't. Maybe that's what has made the difference.

How were the children with each other in the beginning and how have their relationships evolved?

> *Charles:* My three were still grieving the loss of their mom who died three years before I married Mary. Initially the kids stayed pretty tight with their bio-siblings. The two sets of kids treated each other with respect, but there was not much integration. One of the things that we did, sometimes unconsciously, was to make sure there were times when they were all together so they *had* to get to know each other. There are times now when they enjoy each other freely, but if we were to disappear, I doubt there would be much communication between the two sets of children.
>
> We expected we would be a "regular" family. We thought we could establish and enforce consistent rules for all of the children. That is so unrealistic! We had to change our expectations. We eventually accepted that, for instance, each will only take out one dog…not both. Adjust expectations. We had to learn how to be really adaptive. Many times, we've had to *not* have expectations but have *preferences*. One of our family counselors told me to say this: "My preference is…." but be willing to accept that it may not be the way I want. I learned to not make demands about little stuff. We reserve demands for the things we agreed were non-negotiable, even though sometimes we both had to compromise and meet in the middle about those things.

If I knew how hard it was going to be, we may not have done it! Just like the quest for knowledge is a never-ending quest, building a family is a never-ending task. For those who are going into a stepfamily, be prepared to learn every day for the rest of your lives. Every ten years seems to bring a new phase...a new challenge. If you aren't willing to deal with changing issues, you won't be able to help the family succeed. When you work through the difficulties with your children and with each other, it brings a very satisfying feeling.

Mary: The biggest challenge is probably with my own development and the baggage I bring. For example, I tend to take things personally...like when a stepchild doesn't accept me or acts passive-aggressive toward me. I'm the oldest child of an alcoholic. If you know anything about children of alcoholics, you know that we tend to be people-pleasers. When you insert that characteristic into a step-parent, it creates very convoluted interactions. If I didn't have some of those ACA traits, then the things that have been a challenge to me might have been less so. Traits that make any relationship more challenging will be doubly challenging in a stepfamily. *Double at a minimum!*

What do you appreciate the most about each other?

Mary: I appreciate his commitment and willingness to grow and adapt and be loyal...it all fits together. I appreciate what a great role model he is for my children. I have big worries about how they view marriage and women because of what they see from their dad, so I *really* appreciate the example Charles sets. He is very hard working. His willingness to learn and develop has facilitated our working through our issues. He follows through on commitments...does whatever it takes. It's not easy. I know how hard it is to change behaviors!

Charles: I could say about Mary all those things she said about me! I think that first of all, Mary is persistent and won't give up on something she's committed to. She's willing to do the hard, but right thing to succeed. It took a while and it's a continuous process, but I appreciate her acceptance of me with all my baggage—some of which she didn't see before we got married! Along with that, what I love the most is not only *her* ability to grow, but her ability to help *me* grow. She motivates me to change behaviors that have been habitual for 20-30 years by realizing that I don't have to stay the same. When it works to our advantage, I can change. For instance, I went to military schools...was in the military. We tend to be Type As with big egos. Mary's helped me see the positive side of being very forceful and confident, but also helped me recognize that a big ego can be very destructive to a relationship if not managed

KIP AND WENDY:

Kip: When we went through Gordon and Carrie Taylor's class (*Designing Dynamic Stepfamilies: Bringing the Pieces to Peace* is a video based, teach out of the box series), I heard an interview with his son who shared about the struggles he had about his dad getting married. That was the part that got to me. My sons had been indicating reluctance, but I wasn't listening. The combination of that and our personal differences made us decide to just hold off for a while. Even when we got married, I had one son who didn't want anything to do with it. The other three were somewhat on board. They said stuff like, "We see that you've waited, Dad. And you've spent more time talking with us about all of this. We still wish that you and Mom were together. But we understand that's not going to happen so we're OK."

Wendy: My son wanted me to be happy, but shortly after we got married that changed. He didn't like having Kip in the house. Although Kip didn't initiate discipline, he was definitely there to support me. My son felt that he didn't have an advocate. That Kip backed up everything that Mom wanted. Shortly after we got married, he felt he was being mistreated and went to live with his dad. I've had to accept that he's becoming a man and has to figure out his own way in life. My girls were very much in favor of our marriage. They enjoyed being a part of the wedding. Since then, there are occasional glitches, but they really value Kip and what he offers to the family. They definitely see that he brings a lot to me as well as our family.

Kip: If we hadn't gone through the process we did before the wedding—if we were still trying to handle things the way we were before all the classes and counseling—we would already be divorced, or at the least, be miserable!

Wendy: I'm a fighter. I will fight for what's right or to protect someone I love. I fought hard to save my first marriage. That year that we postponed our wedding, when there wasn't an end in sight, I thought, "I'm going to continue to fight for this." Without that year, I think we probably would be miserable and questioning whether we did the right thing by getting married. Instead, because we worked so hard in the beginning, our relationship is rich. We love each other deeply and have a great relationship, not only with each other, but with the kids. Even our relationships with our Exes are better because of the work we've done!

UPDATE 2018: I spoke with Wendy recently. They've now been married for ten years. She reports that she and Kip are each other's best friend. They'd rather be together than spend time with anyone else! The challenges have changed as their children have grown. Now the greatest challenge is being patient and accepting of the choices of their adult children when those choices are not what Kip or Wendy think is best for them. And, that, of course, is the challenge of any parent of adult children. But they have given their children the most valuable gift of a living example of a healthy, loving, lasting marriage.

JIM AND NANCY UPDATE (written about 2002):
I spent a day with Teri collecting medical records and getting pre-op tests shortly before her back surgery. Before we walked into the first of several doctor's offices, she said, "Would it be O.K. if I just introduce you as my mom? You feel like a mom to me today, and I'd be proud to introduce you as my mom, Nancy." Yes!

Dixie was gravely ill during Karen's early teens and died when Karen was 16 years old. Years later I was helping Karen as she was recuperating from Alyssa's difficult birth. She said something like, "I can barely remember my mom before she was sick. You feel like a mom to me. You're the one who's been there to answer questions about being pregnant and nursing. You're there when I have questions or want guidance. You're a mom to me." Sigh.

Steven was 15 years old when we married. Just before his 30th birthday, Steven said something like this to Jim during a treasured conversation held in "guy" territory (the garage) late one night: "You did the best job of being a stepfather that I could ever have asked for. None of my problems were your fault. I'm sorry I hurt you. I'm glad you're there for my Mom. I love you and respect you. I'm grateful you've been there for me, too."

When Peter calls home, he and Jim have long conversations whether I am there or not.

Soon after I "resigned" as a primary parent to Jimmy, I gave him the option of calling me by my first name. As of today, he is 50 years old and I am still "Mom." I feel so blessed to have his love and loyalty after all we put him through. And I'm the one he knows will bake his favorite oatmeal/chocolate chip cookies.

NANCY'S UPDATE 2019:

I occasionally speak to relationship groups, coach couples locally and via the magic of Zoom.us, as far away as Australia and Colorado, write a blog, and am about to finish writing this book, **Stepping TwoGether: Building a Strong Stepfamily.**

My step-daughter Teri lives in Canyon Country, CA. Teri and her brother Jimmy run a residential drug addiction recovery center (Oaks of Hope, www.OaksofHope.com) in Canyon Country, CA along with her husband and two sons. We don't see each other often, but catch up in newsy emails and occasional phone calls.

Karen, her husband Matt and their two children live in Riverside, CA. She helps Teri by doing a lot of the bookkeeping for the recovery program. Recently when I needed a ride to an appointment, Karen volunteered. We ended up spending most of the day together, catching up on news and laughing a lot.

My elder son, Steve, died in 1996 after 15 years of drug abuse ruined his heart. Lessons learned from this precious soul led to the writing of **Pungent Boundaries**, about setting appropriate boundaries and enforcing consequences. Steve spent the last few months of his life clean and sober, earning his own self-respect and my eternal admiration.

My younger son Peter lives with his beautiful wife Shelley in Napa, CA. Both of their children are in college in SoCal. Pete and Shelley recently stayed a couple of days with me. They spent most of one morning doing three big yard maintenance jobs! Pete and I have both worked very hard to heal the wounds he experienced during his teen years. He and his family are a delight to me. Pete has told me several times how much respect he had for Jim. He delivered an eloquent and loving eulogy at Jim's memorial service.

Jimmy, Jim's son, perhaps had it the worst. He was caught in the middle of the conflict that nearly tore Jim and I apart. We didn't get our marriage on good, solid footing until Jimmy was nearly an adult. Jimmy chose a path of drug addiction and many subsequent stays in various prisons until he, in his words, "had a spiritual awakening." For the past few years he has discharged all of his responsibilities to the law, married a wonderful girl, Isabel, who is working with him and his sister Teri to run the drug rehab program in Canyon Country. To Jimmy I am still, "Mom."

CHANGES:

Since Jim's death in 2005, the stepfamily has continued to evolve. We still get together for the big occasions...the weddings of the grandchildren...but don't try to do Christmas or birthdays anymore. One reason is that we all live from one to six hours away from each other. But I believe there is a bigger reason. Jim seemed to be the hub around which we all gravitated. With him gone, the love is still there...there is still a strong connection, but we do not feel as whole as when Jim was here.

The traditions of my own family of origin have changed with the changing ages of the children and grandchildren...and the deaths of my mom and dad. Whether a nuclear family or a stepfamily, times change, needs change, growing families make getting together more difficult. I've concluded that all families are fluid. Over the years some relationships within the family grow closer, others more distant. Then in a few years, the dynamics shift...relationships change.

Stepfamilies in particular are like a fluid puzzle...the pieces keep changing, growing, shifting and evolving. This is normal. Changing circumstances require adjustments.

I recently read, "When life doesn't fit my blueprint, I suffer." An important life skill is flexibility...resiliency. This may be especially true in a stepfamily. Things (plans, parties, get-togethers, living arrangements) rarely stay the same for long. To decide that "if only...then everything would be perfect" is asking for disappointment and pain. Stepfamilies rarely follow an orderly blueprint!

Some things will always remain the same...the commitment to treat each other with respect 24/7, using kind speaking and listening skills, following through with appropriate consequences...but other things...well, just plan to roll with them. Smile.

SUMMARY

Not all of the strategies mapped out in **STEPPING TWOGETHER** are needed in every stepfamily. As you read this book and the experiences of The Cast did any one thing stand out as really making sense? A possible solution to an issue with which you're struggling? Start there. Talk it over with your partner. Are you in agreement? Do you know how to take the next step? Do not try to change too much too quickly. But, starting with your areas of conflict, begin aligning yourselves with the strategies that work best for most stepfamilies...

BUILDING TASK

Take what you've learned here and use whatever you're ready to implement. Talk with your partner about any changes you believe would benefit your stepfamily. Do you agree? Do you need supplemental help learning new communication skills? Would it help to have someone help you prioritize which of these strategies would bring the most benefit?

Coming Next...

Hear what living through the break-up of their parents' marriages and subsequent step-families were like from the view of two step-children...

CHAPTER EIGHTEEN: Stepfamily Kids Speak Out

The persons that are under-represented here are the children who experience living in a stepfamily. Not every child's experience will be the same. The two persons who agreed to share their stories have thoughts and feelings...a perspective... that may be shared by many children, but certainly not all. However, notice the shared feeling of powerlessness, resentment, confusion and overwhelm that Susie and Nathan both experienced. Do you imagine your child or step-child may share some of these feelings?

Susie is Julie's daughter. She's suffered from an anxiety disorder since birth which has made the multitude of transitions in her young life even more difficult. She's a beautiful red-head with a deeply caring heart. Susie was about 18 years old at the time of this interview. Here she poignantly shares about her "three last names" and the men who gave them to her. The first part of this interview was done in 2010.

Susie

> I don't remember much about my birth dad. My mom left him when I was very young because he was threatening to hurt her. When we got older, she would arrange for us to meet him for an hour or two.

> The last time I had contact with my birth-father was in Texas, when I was sixteen. It was a hard age for me. School was tough. I was making a lot of mistakes. But my dad wanted all of his family to meet in Texas for a family reunion. I'd never met any of them. I'd never met my half-sister, Kristen. It took real bravery for me to go and I probably wouldn't have without my brother David with me.

> Yet I enjoyed them. It was fun sitting in the living room joking. In addition to Kristen, he has twins with the woman he went to only two weeks after Mom left him...a boy and a girl.

> It was painful to see him fathering his children...what I missed. I got the impression he was trying to be a real dad while we were there. He took all five of us to get ice cream and a monster drink. I wanted the attention, but it seemed more like a show...like he was playing a role. If he really wanted to be a dad, he would have had more contact with us!

> I asked myself, "What's wrong with *me*? Why couldn't you father *me*?"

> Stepdad #1: He drank a lot and seemed angry a lot of the time. I never considered him a dad. He worked as a firefighter and was gone a lot. I mostly remember that time as being with mom, David and my step-siblings. I loved his children like true siblings. We were together about six years. When we moved to California it felt like these step-sisters were torn from me. We'd been together for about six years. I felt closer to Marie since she came to California with us for a short time. At first it was her

choice, but then she was so different...jealous, lying, so I didn't want her in our family anymore. But it was a big loss for me. I knew she did stuff wrong. I understood, but I didn't want to let go of her.

I was happy when Mom and Ted reconnected. We had fun when he came to Mississippi to visit. I thought he was just a friend. But when Mom said she and (Step-dad #1) were getting a divorce it was a shock. My anxiety was in full swing. It was hard to process these big changes. Ted paid more attention to me than (Step-dad #1) and the move to California was an adventure. We made up a bed in the back seat. That part was fun.

Their wedding was also fun. I was happy about them getting married. I was ten...old enough to get into all the festivities. Ted's family knew my mom, but they didn't know me. A little weird. But I got a new sister and brother! (Ted's children)

By the time I was 12 I began to notice problems. About that time, (2008 when the economy crashed) we lost our house and moved into a rental. On a family trip Thomas, (Ted's son) burped, and I said, "What do you say?" Ted was upset that I "coached" him. Mom and dad (Ted) got in a fight over it. It was the first time I was disciplined by him. A shock. I wondered, "Why is he mad at me?"

THE BIG FIGHT: Sometime later Thomas told mom something (really small) then changed his story when Ted got home. Mom said, "He's lying." We were in the living room, Mom and Ted in kitchen yelling. Dogs barking. It got physical. I was punching, kicking Thomas because I wanted to protect my mom. He tried to get me off of him, and I fell back onto a table. Mom yelled, "He pushed my daughter!" Ted told Thomas to pack his bags because the two of them were leaving. My brother called 911. The cops wanted to talk to all of us together. Ted and Thomas packed and left. They were gone for two days.

What was different was that it was physical for the first time. The verbal fighting was normal for most of the past two years. The beginning as a family was great! Then the rules and fighting began.

(Nancy: A few days later is when I met Ted and Julie at a meeting introducing the marriage classes that were scheduled, then met with them privately to do some emergency coaching.)

After they met with Nancy, I noticed things were better immediately, but I was still mad at Ted. I threw down the tennis racket he gave me. I stayed mad at him until I was about sixteen. It took a long time for me to trust him again. Didn't talk to him for a long time.

At one time Ted told me, "I want to do better with you." I didn't call him dad for a long time, even though David, Thomas and Susie did. Nothing happened immediately. Eventually I was not tense around him anymore.

I'm nineteen now. Now I love Ted! He's more a father figure now than ever. We can talk and laugh together. I'm a little jealous because Ted bonds with Thomas and Annie's sports. But his kids are his kids. Those early years apart robbed us of those bonding times. He is a role model. Lately I realized that all my ex-boyfriends were like my birth or first stepdad. My boyfriend now is more like Ted.

Ted is patient. If I get in a fight with mom, I'll tell him and he'll help me be patient. He's funny. I mainly admire the patience in him. I'm starting to see the qualities I want in a man.

Even though my relationship with Ted is better, there is still a difference between me and his birth-children. It's partly my fault, too. I don't feel like a real daughter. Not 100%. My dad in this life is my grandfather. 100%. He'll forget to say granddaughter, and call me his daughter.

I don't want a stepfamily!!! I know the divorces were mandatory, (life or death) but I want to be 100% sure, because I don't want to go through a divorce. I want to learn, (better relationship skills) not only with my boyfriend, but with others. Some of them I've learned. I know I can be hard-headed. I want to be willing to learn with a whole lot less pain than (Mom and Ted) went through.

ADVICE FOR OTHER STEP-KIDS?

Don't feel pressured to look at the step as your real mom and dad. My aunt has been married four times. I talked with her step-son who asked me, "Why do I have to call her mom?" I told him, "You don't. She's not your mom."

David (Susie's brother) has been more accepting. He says, "Ted's more of a dad to me than anyone else has been so I'll call him dad."

WHAT DO YOU WISH YOU COULD HAVE TOLD YOUR MOM?

Please realize that every single thing that happens affects your kid. Every single fight. I'm not really mad at my mom for all the circumstances I've experienced. I'm kind of grateful that she remained focused on our welfare during all of the chaos. At first, when she married Ted, I resented that I wouldn't have mom's attention 24/7. My anxiety disorder made me needier for her attention...like separation anxiety. They'd leave to go on a date and I'd have a panic attack. I had to share her (with Ted.) But I eventually understood that the relationship with mom and Ted was important and also needed attention.

SUSIE NOW:

Susie was unable to avoid some of the relationship chaos that was the norm for her growing up. She's in a custody battle for her child with a husband that turned out to be a poor choice. She declined my request to give an update for fear her words would jeopardize her case in court.

NATHAN: I met Nathan and his wife, Eva when they attended ***Mastering the Mysteries of Love***[6] class to learn better communication skills. I also was privileged to phone-coach them in practicing the skills. Later Nathan attended ***Stepping TwoGether*** in hopes of understanding his experience growing up in a stepfamily. He was about thirty-five years old at the time of this interview in 2010.

My parents divorced when I was in elementary school. I remember the first time divorce was mentioned. Mom asked, "If we divorce, which one would you want to live with?" Mom regretted that question. I stayed with mom. We rented a room with friends. I spent a lot of time alone. Dad moved

---

Mary Ortwein, MSW, wrote **Mastering the Mysteries of Love**, a simplified derivation of ***Relationship Enhancement*** by Bernard Guerney, Jr while doing relationship research at the University of Pennsylvania. RE has been recognized as the relationship skills program that delivers the highest degree of long-term benefit to couples who go through the program compared to many other programs tested.

to Missouri. I just coped the best I could. At that age (10-12) I guess I didn't know how to express the loss I felt by his moving away.

Three or four years after the divorce mom and Ken (step-dad) began living together. Josh (step-brother) was in his early teens. Mom and Ken got married when I was still in high school. I was very uncomfortable with a new guy in the house. He immediately began exercising authority over me. I might be watching cartoons in the morning. He'd just walk in and change the channel. He had a son that he'd left with son's birth mother (five years younger than Nathan). Now I wonder how much of his behavior was trying to be a father figure, and how much was just his idea of being the man of the house. He was not loving. His attitude was, "I'm the man. Do what I say." If he was outside doing yard work, I had to be outside, too. Or I did the yard work alone.

Neither I nor my dad were good on the phone. I saw him 1-2 times a year when he came to visit the rest of his family. I never thought he came to see just me, but I felt included. I had frequent contact with his mother (paternal grandmother) because she kept me when my mom was working. She has dementia now. But before that I was close to her. She was comfortable. Familiar.

During my teens, my bio-dad's death was a shock, but he was already so far removed from me, I didn't really experience any big sense of loss.

Until the last few years, I felt a lot of resentment toward my step-dad, but now I really love him, and appreciate some of the things he did that helped me be the man I am today. For instance, when I started working at UPS, his advice was "Do whatever your boss tells you to do." He was always a good example of taking care of whatever was needed. If something was wrong with the car or computer, he'd stay up all night fixing it. He was dutiful as a caretaker, though not affectionate.

My relationship with my Mom has always been difficult. I believed that, to her, what I thought or how I felt wasn't acceptable. If mom and I had a difference of opinion, my opinion didn't matter, lacked credibility. Eventually I learned to just shut up. As I was growing up mom would say things like, "The more you act like that the less I love you." Even then I knew it was bull shit...but how could I say that? To express her frustration or hurt, she'd withdraw affection.

I spent most of my teens and early adult life avoiding my step-dad. It seemed like I was the one out of step rather than the family dynamics being out of whack. I didn't realize what an angry person I was until I married Eva. I just thought I had a good sense of humor, but most of my humor was sarcastic, biting comments. My first reaction when triggered by anything was always to be aggressive.

I never challenged Mom and my step-dad, however. It wasn't safe. I might believe that I was being treated unfairly, but mom would back up Ken to convince me that I was the one being inconsiderate. As a teen, I was into professional wrestling. There were two shows, one I liked and one I wasn't interested in. I'm sure my step-dad thought he was being generous to tell me that a pay-per-view was coming up. When I told him, "That's not the show I care about," he expressed anger. He probably felt rejected and thought I wasn't being grateful. I always felt like I was walking on eggshells.

I was buddies with my step-brother, Josh, to begin with, but always on a superficial level. We liked many of the same movies and both loved Halloween. I enjoyed his company because we shared some of the same interests. When I married Eva, she and Josh were jealous of each other and seemed to compete for my attention. Eva tried to control my relationship with stepbrother.

I eventually landed on the side with my wife, so there were several years that Josh was upset with me. He eventually calmed down. I see him couple times a year now. We talk about the same old surface stuff. There's a line there that I know not to cross. We each have strong opinions that we disagree about. If I try to talk about any subject that isn't safe between us, he withdraws…begins playing with his phone. It's not a very vital relationship now. We still love Halloween. We often go to Knott's Scary Farm[7] together to celebrate Halloween.

He's 35 years old and still lives at home. It's a big issue between my mom and stepdad, because stepdad doesn't require Josh to do anything around the house. Josh has free room and board. I realize now that the whole family was somewhat dysfunctional…and still pretty codependent. It's not a place I enjoy spending much time.

Now I live 1 ½ hours away from Mom so I only see her at family functions. She's not a real essential part of my life.

Learning better communication skills (when attending **Mastering the Mysteries of Love** with Eva) and reading **Boundaries** by Townsend and Cloud were defining experiences…like a dividing line or a settling of my past. That book gave me permission to recreate relationships the way I needed them to be. I could do life the way I'd never done it before. I felt released to create life on terms that feel much healthier and right for me. I don't need to get permission from Mom or Ken to live life the way I want to.

Attending **Stepping TwoGether** ushered in more revelations. One thing that stands out is the concept that the birth parents are responsible to parent the bio-child and the stepparent's job to back him/her up. That explained why I felt so much resentment. It felt like Ken was trying to come between me and my mom. I know that wasn't his intention, but that was how it felt at the time. He was just ignorant about how connect with me. It was a different era. They didn't understand stepfamily dynamics.

I had to be away…far removed from the family for several years before I could make a definite change. A few years ago, a situation came to a head that was so black and white that I was able to take a stand. When Eva and I were living in a townhouse, they wouldn't allow pets, so Mom kept my dog. She didn't do a very good job…fed it people food, allowed it to get very obese, wouldn't take it for grooming, etc.

Meanwhile Eva and I bought a house about 1.5 hours away. Anytime the dog needed something she expected me to drive 1.5 hours to her house to take the dog to the vet, etc. Finally, on one visit, when I saw the condition of the dog, I made a decision that I knew wouldn't go over very well. I took her in the back bedroom, away from the other family members, and respectfully said, "It is not my responsibility to take care of the dog if he's living in your house. Either you take better care of him or I'll take him with me to our house."

Knotts Berry Farm is a family theme park in Buena Park, CA. In October they become "Knott's Scary Farm."

She was outraged that I basically issued an ultimatum or boundary. She indignantly said, "Excuse me!" She accused me of being ungrateful (which seems to be the label I'd consistently been given throughout my life.) She stormed into the living room where my step-dad, aunt and others were and said, "Nathan doesn't want to be inconvenienced."

Everyone sided with Mom. I grabbed dog and left. She said it was the end of our relationship. They would never see me again, etc. But slowly the relationship got better, and now the dynamics are very different, much healthier.

Without that defining moment, they wouldn't accept me as an adult…a peer. No matter how many years I'd lived on my own, she would criticize how I did things. That doesn't happen anymore.

That event re-ordered the boundaries between us. It helped me be treated more respectfully as an adult…a peer.

A RECENT UPDATE FROM NATHAN:

I know my mom loved me more than anything else in the world, and I was enjoying the new, more-adult level relationship we now had even though I would always be her "baby boy", however, her unskillful emotional expression for so long before had created a tall wall inside me. I could not trust her with how I really felt or even who I really was, and having lived apart from her with my wife, I found I didn't miss her company. I loved her of course, and could be around her on special occasions to enjoy things on a very basic level.

My mom passed away 9 days after her 65 birthday, 4 days after my Christmas day birthday, about 4-5 years ago now from cancer. Being Christian, she had prayed either God would heal her, or He would take her quickly. She didn't want to go through treatment. Ironically, she had spent most of her adult life addicted to countless prescription medications that had ultimately destroyed her liver and caused the cancer. God chose the latter option and took her very quickly. She had had some undetermined health issues for a couple years, but once she was finally diagnosed with cancer, she was gone in a month.

I know she wasn't happy with her life toward the end, and that had a lot to do with her lifestyle choices of comfort over inconvenience, handicapped by many mental and emotional anxieties she medicated with pharmaceuticals and television—a true couch potato if there ever was one. Though I am thankful for many of the interests in life she instilled in me that I very much enjoy to this day (Halloween, horror movies, Disney, art, etc), and I often fondly reflect back and give credit to her for the life that made me who I am today, I find I don't actually miss her in my life so much as I'm relieved she's no longer suffering and is Home waiting for the rest of the family in Heaven.

Grandma, her mom, has since joined her just a few months shy of her own 100th birthday. And now the maturity that comes with a true realization of mortality has caused me to reflect a lot on my life, who I am, and how I regard what and who I have versus what I think I'm still entitled to. I see this also in the face of my step-dad. My mother's passing changed him.

Since the time of the blow up over the dog, Ken has treated me more as a man, and peer, proud of the man I have become, and always calling me "son." Now he treats me with all the love a father can give a true son. It's a new level of connection to be sure. He remains an undeniable member of my mom's side of the family. He and my aunt, my mom's sister, spent a lot of time together after my mom passed, being the two that probably loved my mom the most, and now they are unofficially a couple minus marriage and the benefits associated with that. Now both retired, they enjoy spending time together, dating, and have annual passes to both Disneyland and Knott's Berry Farm. He's the faithful, dutiful, moral man she never had, and she's the more outgoing woman he needed. I'm happy for them. I never thought it weird, but rather that it made perfect sense.

Now my step-dad is battling prostate cancer. He seems to be winning and has a great doctor and the support of my aunt who feeds him better. I can see the toll it's taking on him, the decline of his prowess and spirit, but he does not indulge in self-pity, and remains loving and generous, and I am happy to still call him Dad and do what I can to love him as the father God wanted me to have.

This has been a tremendous time of reflection and maturing for me as a human being, not just an old boy still trying to cling to the younger days, but a man embracing the phases of life, realizing that each stage has its own wonderful values. We're all going to pass away soon enough, and I'm learning that tomorrow doesn't always stay in the future. Before you know it, it's yesterday, and the people who have always been there aren't anymore. The best place to be is right now, making the most of what I have right now. Fond memories aren't just a thing of the past, but are created every moment I am present with people I love, and who love me.

Tomorrow I'll look back on today. Will I regret that it wasn't as good as my youth? Will I miss it as much as I miss yesterday today? Or can I just be glad I was there, happy for what God has put in my life, and doing my best to make other people's lives, especially my family's lives, worth remembering fondly because I was there, too.

My wife and I had some rough times, and I'm realizing today that much of it was my inability to be present, stuck in the past, waiting for the future, instead of being who she needs right now, the kind of person she's happy was there. I can't expect her to replace what I miss or hope for. I can only accept who she is, and honestly, in her own way, she's an incredible person, and I'm lucky to have her. Where I used to think she was all about changing me, I now know she was just taking care of me. As with my step-dad, the truth wasn't in comparing her to an expectation, but seeing the value in who she's been the whole time, and simply expressing appreciation inwardly and outwardly for the gift God gave me.

Nancy: I am so grateful to Nathan and Susie for sharing their experiences with such candor and grace!

SUMMARY: It's naïve to believe that children will outgrow or "get over" painful events in their lives. The most we can do is use the skills and strategies that are characteristic in the most successful stepfamilies and in the most well-adjusted step-kids to minimize their pain. The things that nurture healing and acceptance for a child are the same things that we, as adults, need to help us move beyond difficult transitions...someone who hears and understands.

BUILDING TASK

Consider reading Susie's or Nathan's story to your child. Ask, "Has your experience been anything like hers? His? What has been the hardest thing for you in this stepfamily? How to you feel about ____?" Then, like Big Bunny, just listen with caring. No judgement or defensiveness. Your child deserves…needs…to have his or her point of view heard and respected. This doesn't mean that you have the power to make everything OK for this child, but just listening and acknowledging the reality of this child's point of view will go a long way toward bringing comfort and healing.

Coming up…An Ongoing Project

CHAPTER NINETEEN: An Ongoing Project

The difficult part of writing a book like this one is that there isn't a clear ending...no obvious Last Chapter. Being in a stepfamily is like beginning a journey without knowing exactly where it will take you.

There are some concrete goals such as learning and using respectful communication skills 24/7. With everyone. Making kindness and affection so habitual that they become part of your character.

But the complex relationships and the evolution of circumstances sometimes lead in directions you couldn't have predicted.

It's sort of like owning a home. The bedrooms serve the kids as long as they live at home. Then someone moves out. You convert that bedroom into a craft room, or a playroom for grandchildren. Eventually you decide to downsize because you don't need all of that space.

In a previous chapter I referred to all families as fluid. They change, grow, readjust.

I have a precious niece named Lori who recently died from a reoccurrence of cancer. She fought valiantly because she wanted to be with her husband, two daughters and extended family as long as possible. But finally, she, and those who love her, had to let go of that hope. She gave us all a spectacular model of dying with grace, but mostly loving to the nth degree for every moment she had left on earth. Her last day here she repeatedly said, "It's all about love! Every lesson on earth is about loving."

I hope that "doing a better job of loving" is the lesson you take from all the information about building a strong stepfamily. Every skill you learn is to help you do a better job of loving and being loved. Every time you Listen with Understanding, it's for the purpose of meeting the speaker's need to be heard. Whenever you join your child or step-child doing a puzzle, or playing catch, or teaching how to bake, or praising that child's bio-parents, you are doing it from love. Every time you schedule a fun date with your partner, or make time for a Skilled Discussion, it's to strengthen your love for each other. Each time you swallow your pride or your desire for loyalty from a step-child, and support that child's relationship with "the other bio-parent," you are practicing love at it's most sacrificial.

Here are some additional resources to help you on your journey of love:

Enroll in the **Millionaire Marriage Club**. There are nineteen 30-minute lessons divided into eight modules that teach loving communication, problem solving, conflict management and relationship building skills. Go to www.NancyLandrum.com for more information and registration. This online program can be done at your own pace and in the privacy of your home.

Make an appointment for a complimentary (free) first appointment with Nancy. Click this link to schedule a time that is convenient for you: https://meetme.so/SpeakwithNancy Sometimes the relationship is so conflicted and the issues so mixed up that neutral, but educated help is needed to figure out how to move forward. There is no obligation to enroll in further coaching after the complimentary appointment.

If you decide to consult a licensed therapist, ask questions! Those not knowledgeable about stepfamily dynamics can do more harm than good. Be sure they have had extra training in stepfamily work.

Purchase **Pungent Boundaries**. If you have a relationship with someone who is struggling with an addiction, or just being very difficult, this short, pithy book may help you decide what you can control and what you can't...and what to do about each category! You can find this book at www.NancyLandrum.com or www.Amazon.com.

Parenting: You may find it helpful to attend a parenting class either with your Ex (to help you co-parent your child) or with your current partner. I like the classes taught by Active Parenting. They have curricula for parenting every age group. There are parenting classes available online although I'm not familiar enough with any of them to offer a recommendation.

Look for a stepfamily support group. Sharing experiences and ideas with other step-couples will be reassuring and inspiring. Or, start a stepfamily support group using this book as your text book! You may find a support group at The Stepfamily Association of America. (https://www.worldvillage.com/stepfamily-association-of-america/) or The National Stepfamily Resource Center, (http://www.stepfamilies.info/about.php)

Email me at Nancy@NancyLandrum.com with feedback about this book and the concepts you've learned here. Share your questions. I'll do my best to respond to every email within 24 hours.

Stepfamilies: Love Marriage, and Parenting in the First Decade. You may find the results of this ten-year study of stepfamilies by Dr. Bray interesting. He confirms that it takes several years for a stepfamily to develop into a family unit...and that stepfamilies coalesce into one of three basic forms. Somewhat scholarly, but easy to read.

Although I've given you all I have in **Stepping TwoGether,** I do not claim that it's a definitive resource for building a strong stepfamily. You will, no doubt, find additional ideas and helpful perspectives by reading or attending other stepfamily resources.

I wish you the very best as you work to create and sustain a loving partner relationship, and together, work to build a strong and loving stepfamily. Please let me know if I can be of further service to you...

Nancy Landrum

Stumbling Blocks to Consistent Progress in our Marriage and Family:
___Taking for granted that the gains we've made are permanent.
___Assuming that we no longer need regular Skilled Discussions.
___going back to old habit patterns.
___Forgetting that as our life-circumstances change, we must find new solutions.
___Neglecting to have regular "couple" times—fun times together.
___Complaining, comparing, blaming.

Building Blocks to Consistent Progress in our Marriage and Family:
___Continuing to practice respectful communication skills until they are habitual.
___Dating regularly.
___Looking for new solutions when new issues arise.
___Attending a Marriage Enrichment class or event every year.
___Being open to learning new things about each other and our relationship.
___Knowing that romance will last as long as we create it.
___Showing appreciation to each other daily.

Not The End!

Made in the USA
Lexington, KY
19 December 2019